RARE BIRDS

RARE BIRDS

Conversations with Legends
of Jazz and Classical Music

Thomas Rain Crowe
with Nan Watkins

University Press of Mississippi · Jackson

www.upress.state.ms.us

Designed by Peter D. Halverson

The University Press of Mississippi is a member of the Association of
American University Presses.

The interviews contained in this collection appeared in whole or part
as the following publications:

"Epiphany As a Rare Bird." *Arts Journal* (July 1990).
"The Holy Terrors (Les Enfants Terribles)." *Nexus* 33, no.1 (1997).
"The Holy Terrors" (edited version). *WP Journal* 26 (Ireland) (1998).
"More Than the Music." *Arts Journal* (Fall 1990).
"Sound Brahman." *Jazz News* 14, no. 94 (1997).
"Sound Brahman" (edited version). *Asheville Poetry Review* (Jazz Issue) 13, no. 1 (2006).
"Transcending the Blues." *Jazz News* 14, no. 98 (1998).
"An African Songbird in New York." *Jazz News* 15, no. 99 (1998).
"A Morning in Paris." *Jazz News* 15, no. 99 (1998).
"Cape Town Love." *Jazz News* 15, no. 102 (1999).

First printing 2008
∞
Library of Congress Cataloging-in-Publication Data

Crowe, Thomas Rain.
  Rare birds : conversations with legends of jazz and classical music / Thomas Rain Crowe with
Nan Watkins.
      p. cm.
  Includes discographies and index.
  ISBN 978-1-60473-103-3 (cloth : alk. paper) — ISBN 978-1-60473-110-1 (pbk. : alk. paper)
  1. Composers—Interviews. 2. Musicians—Interviews. I. Watkins, Nan. II. Title.
  ML385.C73 2008
  780.92'2—dc22
                                                    2008013125
British Library Cataloging-in-Publication Data available

CONTENTS

PREFACE

I t's always tricky writing an introduction to a book of nonfiction, as it is easy to get caught up in one's own intellectual or emotional attachment to the text, which can result in a lot of overblown comments if not unrealistic praise for one's own efforts in addition to what one has written about. I will try, in the following paragraphs, to take my own advice in keeping my uncensored thoughts to a minimum in giving readers a bit of background, as well as a peek at what it is they will find between the covers of this book. If I get a little poetic or rhetorical in the process, forgive me, but this is exciting stuff!

Rare Birds is a collection of six interviews with world-class musicians and composers, all living, contemporary, and active. The list includes Philip Glass, Charles Lloyd, Abdullah Ibrahim, Steve Reich, Eugene Friesen, and Sathima Bea Benjamin. These are in-depth and revealing (candid) conversations that not only focus on banter about the music, but are revelatory in terms of the artists themselves. While Glass and Reich have certainly gotten their fair share of attention for their work, Lloyd, Ibrahim, Benjamin, and Friesen have not received the kind of acclaim and mainstream press that they deserve. In fact, one of the press readers of the early manuscript of this book has written the following lines: "The artists covered in this study are worthy of our attention. The interviews with these otherwise underappreciated jazz artists are valuable, and

I'm glad they are finally getting their due. And the author's conversations with Glass and Reich deal with recent works not covered elsewhere."

Interestingly, if not appropriately for a book being published by a university press located in the South, all of these interviews took place during a time span of ten years—from 1990 to 2000—and almost all of them took place at the Spoleto USA Festival in Charleston, South Carolina. In those years, I was making an annual pilgrimage to the Spoleto Festival while earning a partial living as a freelance writer. Consequently, these interviews appeared in regional, national, and international publications such as *Jazz News*, *The Arts Journal*, *WP Journal* (Ireland), and others.

While books similar to this one may have been published in the past, there certainly has not been one published with this unique combination of high-profile and high-quality artists. And while these are one-of-a-kind individuals and artists, and their work very diverse, there are some common links that bring them together as an indefinable group. Their interest in and pursuit of spirituality, for instance, and their passion for breaking out of the accepted molds of the past with their insistence on always being "new" and "modern," are common ground for all of these artists. In these pages, and in their own voice, they go into depth concerning the creative process and concerning a personal as well as global perspective on the arts. They also address the subject of the human condition, as well as various personal issues apropos to what they are working on musically. While there is much attention paid to musical mechanics, there is equal time given to spiritual and metaphysical concerns and how these more intangible elements of musicality and musical construction enter into the overall process.

These interviews were conducted in very casual conditions, and the matter-of-fact and down-to-earth tone of the comments reflects the situations and the environments in which they were done. This, then, is a collection of conversations rather than formal interviews with prepared questions. The conversations take interesting turns and, at times, unexpectedly veer off into uncharted territory. The results should interest non-musicians and music-lovers as much as musicians and musicologists.

These are six cutting-edge artists ("rare birds," indeed) who have perspectives on the world and on what it is to be both composer and musician that are not usual and are made evident by the quality and originality of their artistic accomplishments. A lengthy discography is provided in addition to each interview to give the reader evidence of each artist's accomplishments and as a way of familiarizing the reader with current releases as well as older titles. In the end, it is my hope that what Nan Watkins and I have done is not only to throw a spotlight on the individuality and uniqueness of each of these artists, but to shine a broader spray of light that will illuminate for the reader the qualities that contribute to each of these artists' greatness, and how they have, in their own unique ways, contributed to, and maybe even changed, the fields of jazz and new classical music.

As a starter for this sumptuous meal that University Press of Mississippi has placed before you, let me introduce you to the Rare Birds sextet:

Vocals: **Sathima Bea Benjamin**—Discovered in 1963 by Duke Ellington in the Club Africana in Zurich and known to many (but perhaps not enough) as "The African Songbird," she has been compared to Billie Holiday and Dinah Washington. Her first CD (which was lost after recording for thirty years until it was discovered and released in 1997) includes musicians Billy Strayhorn, Duke Ellington, and Dollar Brand (Abdullah Ibrahim) and is a modern jazz classic. Today, in her sixties, and one of the jazz genre's best-kept secrets, she continues to record (but rarely performs), adding to her collection of more than twenty albums and CDs.

On cello: **Eugene Friesen**—Known primarily as the long-time cellist for the Paul Winter Consort, he has taken the cello (and the electric cello) into the stratosphere of possibility and cosmic nuances in his solo recordings and in his collaborations with a multitude of modern musicians, dancers, poets, and avant-garde artists. Originally a classically trained cellist who studied at the Yale School

of Music and then immediately became a member of the world-re-
nowned Delos String Quartet, he is one of the most passionate solo
performers of his instrument playing today.

On tenor sax and flutes: **Charles Lloyd**—Thought by many to be
the rightful heir to the throne of John Coltrane, Charles Lloyd took
the jazz world by storm in 1966 with his recording of *Forest Flower*,
which was touted as the first jazz album in the U.S. to sell a million
copies. After playing with such jazz greats as Cannonball Adderley,
Keith Jarrett, Chico Hamilton, Jack DeJohnette, and Cecil McBee,
he struck out on his own, and amidst appearances and disappear-
ances from the scene, he has created a mythos that surrounds him
and his music to this day. Since 1965 he has recorded more than
forty albums and CDs. He has appeared on record with such diverse musicians and groups as The Beach Boys, Jimi Hendrix, The
Doors, Canned Heat, Roger McGuinn, and Mark Isham. A true
jazz legend, Lloyd performs, if sporadically, at festivals and sold-
out concerts throughout the world.

On electronic keyboards: **Philip Glass**—One of the classical
world's truly significant modern composers, he is also considered
(along with Terry Riley, Steve Reich, and a few lesser-known musicians) one of the founders of Minimalism. He has composed for
film, written symphonies, performed as part of small ensembles,
written operas, and is a prolific recording artist. Originally best
known for his operas (*Einstein on the Beach*, *Akhnaten*, *Hydrogen
Jukebox*), he is perhaps better known today from his film scores
(*Koyaanisqatsi*, *The Thin Blue Line*, *Kundun*, *The Hours*, *The Fog
of War*, *The Illusionist*, and *Notes on a Scandal*) for which he has
been nominated for several Oscars.

On piano: **Abdullah Ibrahim**—From South Africa, and originally going by the stage name of Dollar Brand, he was discovered by
Duke Ellington, who produced the recording that would introduce
him to a world audience. Since 1965 he has recorded over one hundred albums and CDs. Known for his soft touch as a keyboardist
and for his haunting rhythms, he is among the aristocracy of jazz
composers and performers—concertizing in halls and festivals all

over the world. After making his home in Europe and then the U.S., at the request of Nelson Mandela he returned to South Africa after the fall of the apartheid regime. He has spent the past several years creating music schools in South Africa, and especially in his hometown of Cape Town.

On drums: **Steve Reich**—After studying in Europe and Asia, he was quickly identified with the World Music scene. He embraced Minimalism and became a household word with the recording and performances of "Different Trains." He has performed with his eighteen-member ensemble in Carnegie Hall and at almost all the major music festivals in the U.S. and Europe. At seventy years of age, he still performs around the world. He has composed many original works for various well-known dance companies. His work has been nominated for several Grammy awards. His minimalist composition "Drumming" has been used and performed by artists and musicians all over the world. Regarded as one of America's premier modern composers, his ten-CD set *Steve Reich: Works 1965–1995* was recently released making him one of the most recorded living American composers.

Enjoy the show.

—Thomas Rain Crowe
Tuckasegee, North Carolina

RARE BIRDS

PHILIP GLASS

Epiphany as a Rare Bird

I look forward to the Spoleto USA Festival every year. Not only because it affords me the opportunity to visit Charleston, South Carolina, which is one of my favorite American cities, but because it lets me witness, firsthand, new performances and productions by some of the world's most talented and provocative artists. In 1990 I was more enthusiastic than ever about my trip from the North Carolina mountains to the South Carolina coast in that I had arranged with the Festival organizers an interview with the American composer Philip Glass on the morning prior to the world premiere of his music theatre mini-opera *Hydrogen Jukebox*.

Hydrogen Jukebox is a two-and-a-half-hour piece of contemporary music theatre whose primary collaborators are composer Philip Glass, poet Allen Ginsberg, and visual design artist Jerome Sirlin. The title of the piece is taken literally from the lines of Ginsberg's magnum opus *Howl*—the book that became a manifesto of sorts for myself and my generation in the late 1950s and 1960s. *Hydrogen Jukebox* contains the "eye-songs," as Ginsberg describes them, of the atomic age. Orchestrated embodiments of what is truly America. An America waking, simultaneously, from both its conscious and its unconscious sleep.

Philip Glass, who is one of the world's most celebrated New Music composers, is also one of the founding fathers, along with Terry Riley, Steve Reich, and La Monte Young, of the Minimalist movement in modern orchestral music. A composer who defines his work in terms of its collaborative content, he has written for opera, orchestra, film, theatre, dance, chorus, and his own group— the Philip Glass Ensemble. Probably best known worldwide for his trilogy of "portrait" operas that include *Einstein on the Beach*,

Satyagraha (which depicts the younger years in the life of Mahatma Gandhi), and *Akhnaten*, Glass has also worked on major collaborative pieces with such artists as filmmakers Godfrey Reggio (*Koyaanisqatsi* and *Powaqqatsi*) and Errol Morris (*The Thin Blue Line*), writers Doris Lessing (*The Making of the Representative for Planet 8*) and David Hwang (*1000 Airplanes on the Roof*), choreographers Twyla Tharp and Jerome Robbins, and most recently with poet/songwriter Leonard Cohen. As a prolific recording artist, Glass is perhaps most well known to the general public for his recording *Songs from Liquid Days* (1985, CBS Records), which features lyrics by Paul Simon, David Byrne, Laurie Anderson, and Suzanne Vega, as well as vocals by Linda Ronstadt.

I knew Allen Ginsberg and spent time with him in the anti–Viet Nam War streets of the early seventies and then in San Francisco in the later years of that same decade. Having spoken with Ginsberg briefly before the May 26 Spoleto Festival premiere of *Hydrogen Jukebox*, I had the chance to sit down later that day with Philip Glass and speak to him, at length, about his music and his work with theatre and opera, the state of the present creative universe, and the future. But, before leaving North Carolina for a Spoleto-injected Charleston, I spent hours listening to all the Philip Glass music I had accumulated over the years. I spent the final few moments before departing writing a concise statement that I thought best described my feeling for Glass's music. A statement that, now, seems like the proper "Glass prologue" for this book as well as an appropriate "fugue" announcing the conversation with him that follows.

If ever the term "future primitive" applied, it applies to the music of Philip Glass. Applies in the portrayal of urban paralysis of rhythmic ecstasy, repetition, and the insinuation of ritual. Glass, or at least his musical vision, seems to come from an intuition of modern mass-insanity driven by the hopeful memory of our deepest archetypal past grounded by the complexly simplistic heartbeat of the Earth.

o o o

In the summer of 1996, I returned to Charleston and the Spoleto USA Festival. This time I went with keyboard musician/composer Nan Watkins, who was prepared to ask Philip Glass the kinds of poignant questions only another musician could ask and that were definitely not a part of my arsenal. The result of her poignancy and presence, I think, inspired Glass to talk philosophically about the Cocteau piece that he was premiering for an American audience (Les Enfants Terribles) and his musical collaborations and compositions.

On June 5, and the morning after the American premiere of *Les Enfants Terribles*, Nan Watkins and I sat with an amazingly bright-eyed and talkative Philip Glass in the courtyard of his hotel in historic Charleston with the intention of talking shop. Instead of the obvious, what we got was something of an interior monologue of not only Glass's philosophical work ethic (oeuvre), but Cocteau's advanced artistic theories about the life and work of The Artist. And all this framed by the troubling and ahead-of-its-time and very Generation X novella, *The Holy Terrors*, as well as by his relationships with contemporary artists and musicians (beginning early on with Andy Warhol and the Beats) who have added their creative signatures to his prolific body of work.

Part I *Hydrogen Jukebox*

THOMAS RAIN CROWE: In looking back at some of your past work prior to *Hydrogen Jukebox*, such as *Koyaanisqatsi, Satyagraha,* and *Akhnaten,* the themes of "truth," "balance," and "reverence for nature" seem to not only predominate, but repeat. Some, like myself, might see these as spiritual preoccupations. Could you speak to me a little about these themes and about how they may, or may not, lie at the center of your work?

PHILIP GLASS: Well, you know, at a certain point I began to see that music with subject matter is the way I work. There are a lot of different ways of categorizing composers. Some of them write or improvise music, and that is one way to do it. Composers are sometimes classified as being either "serious composers of music" or "composers of pop music." And there are composers who work with music in abstract ways and still others who work with music as it is connected to subject matter.

Let's rephrase your question and make it: "What inspires you to write a piece?" For many composers, they simply want to write Symphony #3 or Symphony #4, or Quartet #14, or to write their 3rd Piano Sonata. These kinds of composers are inspired by the language of music itself. And their own development of that language. Then, there are others for whom the inspiration for writing music has nothing, really, to do with music—or at least that is how it would appear. Where subject inspires and dictates the direction of any new music. Something in subject, for instance, like "social change through non-violence" or "an ecologically balanced environment." It's a rather small number of composers among the whole general run of composers who are so attracted to subject matter. I happen to be one of those.

By and large, composers with strong interest for subject matter end up working in the theatre. When I first began working in the theatre in 1965, I first began by working with experimental theatre companies. Working in a somewhat literary tradition. With people whose work was inspired by Beckett, and even Brecht—whose work was a little more involved with social consciousness, even though not in ways that would be recognizable as such to us today. It was really when I began working on my own pieces in the mid-1970s beginning with *Einstein on the Beach* that I really began to think seriously about just what the pieces were about. Or, put another way, when you start to write an opera, or even a piece like *Hydrogen Jukebox*—which is a small opera—it can take about a year and a half to do a small piece, and a large piece may take as long as two to three years. So, for me to spend that much time working on a project, it has to be about something that's important to me.

Here's an example. I worked with [Nobel Laureate] Doris Lessing on a book of hers called *The Making of the Representative for Planet 8*. It's the story of a civilization which is living on another planet called Planet 8. A planet which is about to enter an ice age. And everyone on the planet, the whole civilization, is going to disappear. The whole book is about how the people of Planet 8 address the question of survival. Of course it's clear from the outset that this is an allegorical story and all the things that come up in the story are things that have to do with the world we live in today. As there are very many of us here on our planet that think that we could very well be on the edge of a catastrophe or even a disaster of global proportions. So we worked together for almost three years preparing this book which absorbed a lot of my time, yet it was possible for me to do that with an unflagging interest. I never got tired of working on it because the issues seemed so urgent. So important were these issues that it went beyond my interests as an artist and how I develop and became a project embracing a much larger social context.

As I get older, I find that in order to gear up in order to do the big pieces, I really have to feel that this is something that has *that* much scale to it, that has that much weight to it. For instance, I did another piece not too long ago with the filmmaker Errol Morris called *The Thin Blue Line*, which is a very simple film, in a way, about a man who was wrongfully jailed for a crime he did not commit. In this case, a very simple example of injustice to only one person which is not of the scale of the film I did with Godfrey Reggio called *Koyaanisqatsi*. *Koyaanisqatsi* is a film in images—without words or character—which is presented as a portrait of America. Specifically as it experiences the impact of a new high-tech society. Of a new high-tech culture. So, it's the story of the impact of high-tech culture on contemporary society. *Koyaanisqatsi* is a film about a whole society coming to terms with a new way of living and was a small project in that I was only involved with it for four or five months. But even the small projects, for me to get interested in them, and to do my best work, they have to have something as compelling as these about them in terms of subject matter.

It seems to have intensified as I've gotten older—this need to find a point of departure for the work. A point of departure which springs from a concern for the world I live in in a very ordinary way. The ordinary world that we ordinary people live in in an ordinary way. All those things. The ordinary world we wake up in and to and what's happening to it.

Hydrogen Jukebox, of course, was an ideal project in that way. Allen Ginsberg's work has ranged and roamed over these subjects for thirty-five years. There's no one who has been more at the center of the major issues of our time than Allen. To the point that things that seemed so radical in the sixties almost now seem like mainstream issues.

CROWE: There's an idea that I've been carrying around with me since I was very young, and that is: that there is a direct sympathy between sound and color. Between sound, color, and language, in fact. And that this "sympathy" or synchronicity applies, further, as well to movement and dance. It boils down, ultimately, I suppose, to a question of notation and transmission and how artists in these different fields of creativity experience and record their work. And I'm wondering whether or not major works, for example, excerpted from each of the creative disciplines would be saying the same things, cross-translatively? If Beethoven's *Fifth*, for instance, were somehow translated, note by note, into any spoken or written language, what would that "poem" say? What would the painting look like? How would the dancer move?

GLASS: Yes, this is an interesting idea that other people have had, too. Scriabin for instance, had the idea of the association of color with music. I believe that Messiaen was also interested in this idea. Look into it, it's fascinating. Scriabin actually spent a lot of time and thought-energy trying to find real correlations between the two. I think his work on this subject would interest you, especially.

My work, generally speaking, is collaborative. So, I'm working with other artists all the time in similar kinds of ways to the things you've mentioned. With dance, design, literary sources . . . As well as quite literally with light in the form of lighting techniques. All the music theatre work I have done up to this point includes all these things. So, you might say, I've been placed in an opportune way to see how that happens. And my personal view of all this is that very often these things are contributing aspects to a total work. And that by themselves they don't really "do it." What we look for in a theatre piece when we bring these things together is something that is *more* than the sum of its parts. In that sense very often we're not looking to reinforce things. In other words, I don't look for a visual complement that reinforces a musical statement. I'm usually looking for something that is different. That actually heightens the music and heightens the image at the same time because they are different and *not* the same. This happens in film all the time.

Let me give you an example of what I'm getting at. Again, with the film *Koyaanisqatsi*, there were scenes where the music and the images act on each other to activate different aspects of each other without actually complementing each other, or, as I say, reinforcing each other. For instance, early on in the film there is a scene where you see these huge airplanes floating down onto the runway. Floating in the air. This is directly followed by scenes dominated by tanks, warplanes, and cars. This was a section of the film we called "vessels"—meaning things that you travel in, like a boat. Writing the music to go with the visual images on the planes, the tanks, and the cars, I decided to concentrate on one aspect of those things. Looking at the planes, I took the idea of "lightness" and I set it for voices. So, in the finished product, the opening scene with the montage of the airplanes is done to six-part a cappella choir. So I took one aspect of the image, which was the image of floating, and created a musical sound that, to me, insinuated floating. But I could have done it many different ways. There are other places in the film where I reinforced the images directly. Later on in the piece there is a whole segment of rapid movement of a variety of things. Here, I used a very rapidly moving music. A very simple one-on-one association was used in this case—a musical technique mirroring a visual technique. There is a way to reinforce something by similarity and there is also a way to reinforce something by dissimilarity. In other words, you can go against the image or you can go with the image.

In *Hydrogen Jukebox* we have used this technique of dissimilarity quite a bit. In fact, very seldom did we use the complementary approach in combining all three elements of the piece.

But to get back to your question—it may be that these seemingly dissimilar things are actually saying the same thing, but in different mediums. *But,* when you put them together it's better not to treat them that way. In other words, even if it's true, if all they do is reinforce each other, you end up with an overwhelming one-dimensional work. Let's say that a certain color combination may give a certain emotional ambiance, and a certain chord combination may give a similar emotional ambiance—the fact that they're the same or at least similar to each other doesn't mean that they go well together. They might *not* go well together. In creating a performance piece such as *Jukebox* you really have to entertain the whole range of possibilities.

CROWE: All this talk of similarity and dissimilarity as a means of combining and unifying things brings to mind some of the more recent advances in the field of theoretical physics. Especially the notion of a "unified field theory" whereas it pertains to the notions of "order in chaos." Somehow your music theatre creations would seem to be artistic attempts at coming up with the same "formula" as are these theoretical scientists. That your collaborative process, and maybe even the results, are in themselves mini unified field theories played out onstage through the vehicle of "the arts." What would you say to this hypothesis?

GLASS: Well, I think this notion of unified field theory and all might be stretching it a little. But there is something to what you are saying. Let me answer you this way: When we began with the idea of *Hydrogen Jukebox,* Allen might have come up to me and asked: "Why do you want to take my poetry and set it to music?" This is a good question. In fact, Doris Lessing did say this to me. In her case it was: "Why do you want to take my novel (*The Making of the Representative for Planet 8*) and make it into an opera?" What both Doris and Allen are asking is: What are you doing for the work? What I said to Doris in response to her question was: "I can do things in the music that you can't do in the words. I can describe things that your words describe, but I can do it in a way that the words can't do it." In terms of Allen's poetry, I am reminded of a writer by the name of Edward T. Cone whose book I just recently finished. In his book on "words and music" he says when you set words to music you are making one interpretation of all the possible interpretations. And so in a certain way by doing this you are limiting it. You have defined it in a way. But, on the other hand, he goes on to say—and this is the point that I wanted to make—he says that what you get, instead, is a *vivid* presentation. Something more vivid than either the music or the text would have by itself. The word "vivid" is central to the appropriate response to this question. It comes from the root word "vive"—meaning: to live; liveliness.

CROWE: Would this include the idea of "epiphany"?

GLASS: Well, epiphany is certainly a part of vividness. Hopefully, though, epiphanies are rare birds—not flying into the room every day! I've had a few artistic ones, and I've talked to Allen and he's had some. Most artists, in fact, will tell you about epiphanies they've had. Realizations that have come out of a heightened experience. A heightened emotional experience. And the vividness of that can sometimes lead to an artistic insight, or even to an artistic quest that may last as long as twenty or thirty years. On the other hand, you may try and create through your own art form an epiphany that you had when you were a child. Actually, that's literally what happened to Allen. He had an epiphany, a vision, in his early twenties and he says that much of his writing is an attempt to recreate that.

But to get back to your original question . . . What music *can* do in a general way is to heighten our emotional sensitivity and awareness. And when applied to a particular subject, it can bring that heightened perception to the subject, itself. So, if I set a poem of Allen's to music, from that point on you, as the listener, might remember that poem more easily because it may have a whole emotional world attached to it, now, through the music.

CROWE: Something along the lines of what Wagner was doing?

GLASS: Yes, and maybe Schubert. He was another good example, here. Sometimes maybe not thought of in the same way, but in truth he was working in very much the same way as Wagner in terms of combining music and language.

Again, we're back again to the idea of why it is that we do these things such as creating new music-theatre operas. These kinds of questions are multifaceted. There are a lot of reasons, really, why we do these things. We have talked about social issues on the one hand, but there is this other aspect of bringing things to a kind of heightened experience of awareness. Aristotle, for example, talks about "catharsis" in tragedy in the *Poetics*. He describes it in a way that would be very close to epiphany and what we are calling, today, this kind of "vividness" in the work. There are many younger artists—and even some of us older ones—who are attempting to arrive at this state in a variety of ways. Athletics, in fact, approaches this. Long-distance runners and weight lifters are good examples here. Weight lifting, although very physical, is also primarily a mental thing. We're talking about heightened states of awareness here, and there are many people who don't think they are interested in art and so gravitate toward athletics, instead. But I'm not so sure that these kinds of interests, whether it be in art or in athletics, are that different.

CROWE: My experience with your music is that there is a kind of contradictory calm, an impending groundedness, amidst the inherent chaos and implied stress in some of your scores and albums. How would you react to this assessment of your music? Or, maybe, this *is* the whole point of your work!? Is it possible that the kind of subliminal "calm" I am experiencing in your work is really a conscious effort on your part to create an "eye in the middle of the storm" phenomenon which may in some way be something of a psychic "direction marker" for the masses?

GLASS: I'm having a little difficulty with your question in the sense that it implies that the object of my intentions as a writer and performer of music is didactic in purpose. That the conscious purpose foremost in my mind is that music and the creation of music is somehow primarily part of a teaching role. And even though this may be true functionally in some ways, the bulk of my intentions is much more innocent than that. What I do and the way that I go about it has to do with my own perceptions about such things as the social issues we were talking about earlier. Luckily, I would say, a lot of people are also interested in the things I get interested in and so are attracted to it. In this way some of my pieces may synchronistically become kind of teaching vehicles in some way for some people.

Again, a good example is the film *Koyaanisqatsi*. The reason I became involved in making the film is because I was very interested in what Godfrey Reggio was doing. It was fascinating for me, personally. I got involved because of this interest or fascination, not because I thought it could or would change the world. I loved what Godfrey was doing and I wanted to be involved. As it turned out, I think that the film does have some redeeming social value, and so was helpful to "the cause of heightened awareness," if you will.

I think maybe it's important to say here that I am, also, in the same position as the listener. I'm not that different from the listener. In other words, what I am exposing to myself can very often be new to me. In a way, I'm proceeding from a position of ignorance, which I am overcoming like everyone else. When Godfrey and I went around for a time talking to people about the film *Koyaanisqatsi*, people were always asking him what he meant by this and what he meant by that, referring to the film. He was always careful to respond to these questions by saying, "Well, you know, the question is really more important than the answer. I can frame the question, but I don't know the answer." Although he saw some of the problems of the impact of a high-tech culture on contemporary society, he was quick to say that he didn't have any answers to these questions. He was very careful not to set himself up as some sort of messiah. And I think that we try and do that in this culture to our heroes. We think that they know more than they can reasonably be expected to. I think that that kind of modesty is appropriate as an honest assessment of where we both were in relation to the making of the film.

So, to get back to your idea about the calm or centeredness in my music and whether or not that is meant to be a sign to other people—as I say, the music doesn't proceed from the idea of the sharing of a great spiritual insight. It doesn't. I'm in the same position as everyone else in that I am trying to break through my own limitations. And what you are seeing in *Einstein on the Beach*, *Koyaanisqatsi*, or *Hydrogen Jukebox*, is me doing that.

CROWE: In your recently published autobiographical book *Music by Philip Glass* [Harper & Row, 1988], I remember you speaking of expectations. Of others' expectations of us, and of our expectations of ourselves. And you go a little further by talking about the notion of "going beyond what we expect of ourselves." I was very interested in reading what you had to say on that subject, which would seem to fit in here with this conversation we are having about creativity and integrity of intention. Could we talk a little more specifically, here, about the notion of "going *beyond* what we expect of ourselves," and the importance of that?

GLASS: I don't know if I'm bending the subject to current affairs here, but right now so much of what's disturbing to artists is the issue of the enemies of the National Endowment and free expression in the arts. In our community and in our society we have people who are very much afraid to "go beyond themselves." When artists like Mapplethorpe or Ginsberg start to work along the frontiers of what those people consider acceptable, they consider it very threatening. They have a hard time understanding what these breakthrough artists are doing. They think that they are actually trying to destroy the world they're living in, and in a certain sense they're not far wrong. Because what someone like Ginsberg or Burroughs or Mapplethorpe are trying to do is to move the center to a different place. And this does mean breaking down the invisible borders of our minds. But here the important thing to remember is that, first of all, these people, these artists, are challenging themselves. It turns out that what they are doing may challenge other people, too. But the history of art has always been that way.

We, today, only have to go back a short time to witness these kinds of things, these kinds of public attitudes toward the arts. To go back and look at people like Jackson Pollock or Willem de Kooning or Andy Warhol. People not all that long ago thought that Andy Warhol was making fun of them. Not that Andy wasn't having a good time, mind you.

So, we have in our culture the people who don't want to change it and are afraid of the change. It's threatening. It's disturbing. They can barely hang on to what they've got and here's some jackass come along who's trying to turn everything upside down. And in a certain way you can have a certain sympathy for that kind of attitude, because not everyone has the capability of absorbing these kinds of changes. Even so, this kind of attitude is anathema to the artist as it is a direct threat to the lifeblood idea of going beyond ourselves, or what we expect of ourselves. These kinds of attitudes not only are hurdles but can become actual walls or barriers to our attempts at overcoming our own ignorance, at exploring the unknown.

CROWE: I was delighted to read in your book that "the operatic tradition seemed to me hopelessly dead in the world of performance in which I worked . . . I don't doubt that the world of traditional repertory opera will eventually be dragged—probably screaming—into the twentieth century with the rest of us." This has, too, always been wishfully my feeling (much to the discomfort of my opera-loving friends!). Could you explain the basis for your statement from the book as well as anything from your experience in the theatre in more recent years which might support, more specifically, this idea?

GLASS: I tend to look at this through my own narrow point of view. But one of the big things—which I went into in great depth in the book—is the collaboration. The interfacing of artists in a different way than what you find, or would have found, in the process of creating opera in the old tradition. An interfacing of artists where the artistic vision can be a spontaneous result of people working together as opposed to the kind of "master overview" of the vision of one person. We have plenty of examples of this more limiting kind of "collaboration" in the nineteenth century.

We, and when I use the word "we" I mean *my* generation, we're not against the old operas—some of them are very beautiful. It's just that at this point and to me there doesn't seem any point in doing them like that anymore. I don't think we're interested in that. In terms of process whereas collaboration is concerned, a lot of it has to do with technology. The new technology has allowed us, somewhat paradoxically, to bring the arts together in a way that we could have never done before. *Hydrogen Jukebox* is a perfect example of this, with its amplified stage projections, images, amplified music, vocal music, etc. During the process of making this piece, I have often wondered how, in fact, we could have even put on this piece two hundred years ago. Not only we couldn't have, but we wouldn't have even of thought of it! The technology available to us now gives us that opportunity. It allows us this possibility.

I don't think that you can underestimate the effect of technology on artists today. It's literally opening up and determining new ways of working. I don't think that we'll ever go back. And in truth you can't ever go back to old forms.

How technology has impacted my work personally is that when I work as a musician I have two or three people that work with me. There is someone who works as a music director, who works on synthesizers developing sounds which are tailor-made for each new piece. We work together developing the technology for the sounds. I simply don't have the time to do all this by myself. The man-hours involved in mastering these technologies is beyond what one person is capable of doing.

It's probably not stretching it to make the comparison that what is going on today in music theatre is comparable to collaborations during the Renaissance. With small armies of artisans and apprentices working together to produce these large-scale performance events. In the case of my work, these people with whom I work are not apprentices, but co-workers working with me to create new pieces. *Koyaanisqatsi*, again, is a good example of this. If you pay attention to the credits for this film at the end of the film, they go on for about four minutes! While this film might be the vision of only a few people, it is not the complete work of only those few. It is the work of many. And through this process it becomes, finally, a vision that is shared by many.

I think that the movement toward collaborative work has mainly to do with the vistas of technology and the simple fact of man-hours and manpower that's needed to dominate the technology and make it work the way you want it to. I dare say that one person could not be accomplishing, could not have accomplished, the work that I have done. It does take a group of people. People are always asking me "how do you do so much work?!" And I say, "I don't." I have a bunch of people I work with—up to a dozen. Practically the only thing I do alone is at the beginning of the day when I sit down by myself to compose. Otherwise, I'm working as part of a team.

Writing the score is the beginning of a long road which will finally lead to a production. The ability to coordinate these new forms, to bring in people, to work with a visual artist such as Jerome Sirlin, or a lighting designer who can work miracles when you need them, all becomes part of the extended work of "composing." Of putting together the pieces of a total production.

I think we're pushing more and more towards something which I think for us has become an ideal—which is a kind of collective work. Where art and technology are finally working hand in hand. And through the labor of all these people working together, a piece like *Hydrogen Jukebox* is possible even though it takes an enormous amount of collective and individual talent. It's impossible to conceive of doing something like this in any other way.

CROWE: And what about the idea that music theatre is becoming the opera of the future?

GLASS: Well, the truth is that this is all happening in the *present*. Music theatre has, I believe, *become* the performing art of choice of the theatregoing public. *1000 Airplanes on the Roof* went to seventy cities. We did one hundred and fifty performances in eighteen months. Fifty-five cities in America which included a performance in your state of North Carolina. We couldn't have done such an extensive tour with this piece were there not the support from people attending the performances. So, music theatre is something that's happening in the present and will continue to happen with more frequency in the future. *Hydrogen Jukebox*, I expect, will also travel around the country. Our only limitation, now, is not audiences—the audiences are there—but the question of how portable we can make the piece. Here again we are back to technology. We have to figure out how to take this piece and get it on the road. How to get it into a truck and how to get the set built in eight hours so we can do a show in one city one day then move to another city the next day and do it again. But the public is there. The appetite and interest is there.

CROWE: Since we are speaking of the ends of things . . ..In your opera *Akhnaten* (which is part of a trilogy which includes *Einstein on the Beach* and *Satyagraha* focusing on the early years of Gandhi), the scribe appears out of the chaos to announce the end of Akhnaten's reign. In *Hydrogen Jukebox*, the scribe (the poet) Ginsberg emerges three thousand years later amidst chaos to announce the end of the reign of, what?

GLASS: Most literally in *Hydrogen Jukebox* where Allen appears in the performance is at the end of the first act in song #10 which is taken from his poem "Wichita Vortex Sutra," where we use a recording of his voice reciting the poem—or more to the point: performing the poem, as the recording is much more than a recitation. This is the only time during the performance that this is done. So the most direct answer to your question would probably have to come from the text of "Wichita Vortex Sutra" itself. Otherwise, I might add that things in general look pretty bad. But Allen, I think, is more pessimistic than I. I hold out a little hope. Hope that is based, mainly, on examples of things that *are* getting better. In terms of environmental issues there are examples such as Lake Erie where after years of such bad pollution that nothing could live in that body of water, recently there is evidence again of fish life. Closer to home, for me, in the Hudson River, the water quality has improved to a point where there are fish again living in this river. These are just two examples, and there are other examples of improvements on the environmental front. These small examples, as minor as they are in the overall drama of things in general, are still indications to me that things can be turned around and past mistakes rectified.

Despite these signs of recovery, the overall picture is grim, I admit, but at least some of these issues—which have been at the center of Allen's work all along—are beginning to be addressed in large-scale serious kinds of ways. Or at least that's what we are being led to believe. One can only hope that this, in fact, is what is happening. We'll see.

CROWE: You have mentioned in numerous interviews and in your recent book that in the early 1970s, theatre—specifically the work of Brecht and Beckett—-had a profound effect on your music. For me it was, early on, dance—which carried over as the "movement of language"—that inspired and excited me. Then it later became music (rhythm), largely inspired by my experiences of Native American drumming and singing, that began to "fire" my words. What is it *now* that might have such a formative effect on your thinking or on your creation of music?

GLASS: When I was younger, it was the visual arts that caught my attention. I was mostly inspired by painters and sculptors. Later, like yourself, by dancers. Now, I'm actually more interested in writers. I'm coming around to writers. To people like Allen Ginsberg and Doris Lessing, and even some younger writers. I'm discovering a new magic in poetry and language that is finding its way into my music. For the last couple of years I've been working almost exclusively with writers on major collaborative pieces. This past year, for example, Allen and I have been traveling around the country performing together as something of a sideline to this larger work we have been working on called *Hydrogen Jukebox*. I'm beginning to find (as Edward T. Cone says in his book) that it's true, at least for me, that music and language are inherently similar and compatible in ways that are not only interesting, but inspiring. And so this is the direction my work has taken.

CROWE: In San Francisco during the mid-1970s, there was a group of poets and artists—of which I was one—connected with the resurrection of *Beatitude* magazine. The media and the community were calling us "the Baby Beats." There's a whole new generation coming up now since the late sixties, early seventies and your first performances and the advent of "minimalism" and "New Music" as it is called. Who, if any, are the "Mini-Minimalists," the pioneering new composers of an even newer "new" music? Can you tell at this point in time what will be the "new" music of the twenty-first century?

GLASS: Let me just say at the outset that I am always reluctant to name names of young people because it can be a big burden for them. And then there is the problem of forgetfully leaving out the names of others equally as talented or important. You understand? But, in response to your question: Yes, they do exist. Living in New York City as I do, I am able to see a lot of what's going on around the country and the world. Everything, it seems, eventually makes its ways from Texas and Nebraska and Maryland, to New York. And so living in New York, despite the fact that it is a difficult city to live in, does have its advantages. And one of the advantages for me I've found is that it is not a bad place to see things happen.

In terms of what directions I see music taking . . . ? For one thing I think it will continue in the area of mixed media. The sort of things we've been talking about. One of the things that is happening to bring this about is the fact that the technology is getting cheaper. I think you'll find in the near future that the reaction to all these big pieces we're doing is to see smaller, easily affordable pieces done in new ways. One of the things that's going to happen is that because of the new affordability of this new technology, it will become possible for new artists to make pieces in their own apartments and backyards, and be able to travel easily with these pieces. Even now, there are younger composers in England who have virtually made recording studios in their apartments for as little as four or five thousand dollars. Sampler, tape machine, keyboard controller, and they're off! . . . I'm also seeing people beginning to put together theatre companies where before the costs for such ideas were restrictive. So, what has been missing in the past twenty years or more has been the means for young people who don't have the means, to start. Which is what I did.

So, with the new affordable technology these younger composers will develop new techniques and a new kind of language to go with what they can do with this new technology. I'm already beginning to see this happen. That there are new musical and theatrical levels developing around these kinds of guerrilla stripped-down outfits. And it's interesting. And what will happen to them as they acquire the means to expand will be interesting to see. But there are already a lot of places in the New York area where you'll see young people working with, not primitive equipment, but with very sophisticated equipment that they have been able to get their hands on with very little money. So, I think we're going to see a reaction to all this high-tech stuff, but in the context of a new kind of technology. Still high-tech, but simpler. Portable. And I think that there is a tremendous amount of room in the future for gifted and imaginative people to still be able to work.

Part II *Les enfants terribles*

CROWE: It's hard to believe that it's been six years since we last talked here in Charleston, but it has, and so I'd like to pick up our conversation where we left off—with you talking a little about the profound influence that writers have had on your work in recent years.

Specifically and appropriately for your Spoleto/American premiere of *Les enfants terribles* last evening, I'd like to ask you about how you came to be interested in the work of Cocteau, who was, especially at a younger age, a major influence as well upon my work.

GLASS: I probably saw the movies that I have worked on within this trilogy (*Orphee*, *La belle et la bete*, *Les enfants terribles*) when they were new. Which would probably be around 1952 or 1953. And if not new, very close to being new. That would have made me fifteen or sixteen years old. Living in Chicago.

I remember there was a little theatre—the Hyde Park Theatre—that used to play movies with subtitles. In those days there were very few movie theatres that did that. In fact, at that time, that was probably the *only* theatre in Chicago that you could see movies with subtitles. And I saw these three movies at that time. They made a big impression on me. Not long after I had seen the Cocteau films, I went to Paris for one summer as a young man. This gave me the opportunity to see for myself the kind of world that Cocteau lived in. In fact, he was still alive and living there at the time. And, of course, at that time I didn't have a clue that one day I would be working with his cinematic material. I was a seventeen-year-old kid. I wouldn't have even been vaguely thinking in these terms, including whether or not I might be able to meet Cocteau. However, looking back now, I wish I had been more conscious and inquisitive about the work of Cocteau as well as Cocteau the man.

I went back to live in Paris in the 1960s. Cocteau was still alive. I didn't meet him then either. So, I had two chances to meet him, I suppose, but it was really just a matter of us being in the same place at the same time. Nothing more.

It wasn't really until the late 1980s or early 1990s, about the time that you and I met when I was here [at the Spoleto Festival USA in Charleston] for *Hydrogen Jukebox*, that I got the idea and was working on the beginning stages of the first piece of the trilogy, *Orpheus*. I had the idea to begin a series of pieces, operas, that were based on film. My thinking was, that opera has always been based on the literature of its time—poems, plays, novels—and oddly enough it was right around the one hundredth anniversary of the beginnings of film, which by 1990 had become almost another kind of literature. Up to this point, I couldn't think of anyone who had taken a film and turned it into an opera—or worked in the reverse process. There had been people who had made films out of operas, but none that had made an opera out of film.

I remember thinking that this fact was very odd. Why no one had used the most influential art form of the twentieth century as a basis for work in other mediums. And so once I had fixed on this idea, the movement toward the work of Cocteau became a natural thing for me. Cocteau was a writer, a poet, a playwright, a painter, and a filmmaker. He was an artist who approached film as an art form. I think in his day people criticized Cocteau. They felt because he did too many things that he was, therefore, a kind of dilettante. I don't, of course, look at it that way at all. My perception was at the time, and still is, that Cocteau was doing one thing, really, just do-ing it in several different ways. I think his subject matter has always been, put simply, the process by which we transform the ordinary world into a world of magic and transcendence. *That* is the subject matter of Cocteau! And everything that he does is about that. He single-mindedly was working in this way. And besides that, I think that because of the focus of his work and the different ways which he approached it, one almost has to come to the conclusion that he was one of the most profound artists, thinkers, philosophers of the twentieth century.

I think of him, and especially in some of his lighter works, as sort of hiding himself behind his work. For example, in *La belle et la bete*, he would say, "This is just a fairy tale, for children." He was constantly hiding behind his work, inconspicuously. But if you look more carefully, you begin to see how his philosophical or spiritual ideas are expressed in the work. *Le belle et la bete*, *Orphee*, *Les enfants* are primary works which exhibit this posture. And these are the three Cocteau pieces that I remembered from childhood, and knew the best—which is why, I'm sure, that I chose them as the three parts of the Cocteau trilogy, and wanted to do them as opera.

In each of these three Cocteau pieces, the question of creativity is predominant. In each of the three films he asks "the question." And not only does he ask the question, he has the good manners to give you an answer. Answers to the question of creativity. I know many more people who also ask questions, but don't know the answers. Cocteau had an answer. For example, the question in *Orpheus* was: "How does the poet become immortal?" The answer is right there in the film where Heurtebise is talking to the princess and they're about to send Orpheus back in time to be with his wife [Eurydice] and Orpheus says, "This is the one thing that we can't do. We can't go back in time. Think about what it is you're doing. Think about the penalty of such a thing!"

Interestingly enough, I was working—around this same time that I was contemplating the Orpheus piece—on a piece with Stephen Hawking called *A Brief History of Time*. One of the basic premises of Hawking's theories of quantum mechanics and of the film made about his life and ideas, is that the arrow of time only points in one direction. Which is just what Orpheus is saying about this idea of his being sent back in time!

However, Heurtebise's response to Orpheus's objection to being sent back in time was, "In order for a poet to become immortal, a sacrifice has to be made." In this case, the sacrifice is the character of Death giving up her love for Cocteau, or Orpheus, in this case— which, in reality are both one and the same. So, she gives up her love, and by surrendering her love, Orpheus becomes immortal— which is something of a paraphrasing of the Shakespearean sonnet "And Death once dead, there's no more dying then." However, what does Death do to Orpheus in that moment in the film? She kills him. What's behind this action is the idea that the way you bring a dead man back to life is by killing him! And Death once dead, there's no more dying then . . . .

With *La belle et la bete* . . . very interesting! Here the question is: "What are the qualities that are required for transformation to take place?" This is a very interesting question! If you are a young artist or composer and you're searching for a wise old person with the questions about what is required for a work of art to be made, Cocteau has the answer to these kinds of questions in the scene when La Belle (Beauty) is about to go back to her father, to leave La Bete (the Beast). . . . And there's this great scene in the garden by the spring where the Beast says, "All my power comes from magic; and the magic comes from five elements: the horse, the rose, the key, the glove, and the mirror."

Here, the horse represents strength and determination. The key represents technique. The mirror represents the pathway—the path from here to there. The rose is the goal. In other words, if you wanted to go from Charleston to Asheville, you would have to know the road, know where you're going, have a way of getting there, plus, have the strength and determination to get you there. And, of course, the natural ability. Then, there's the glove. . . . And I puzzled over this one for a long time, trying to come to terms with its symbolic context in this film. Then it finally struck me—the glove represents nobility. Cocteau is saying two things here. One, that the artist is a kind of nobility; but he's also saying that the pride of the artist is also essential. And by pride I don't mean arrogance, I mean the private space we come from.

So, these are all the qualities that one needs, according to Cocteau, in order to be creative. But even with all of these magical properties, the Beast is still the Beast. He doesn't become transformed into the prince until Beauty gives him the "look of love." The "glance of love." So, there is actually a sixth thing that is required. And the sixth element essential for transformation is "the look of love." And Cocteau is not talking about ordinary love, here. Rather, he is referring to a love that is not possessive. It's the love of generosity. And so the Beast tells her that she is free to go back to her father. You see, it is only when La Bete treats her with the love of generosity that La Belle returns the love. And the foundation for the Beast's transformation is set.

This is all very interesting, and as well, informative! Information essential for any young artist. Cocteau is spelling it out in this story. He says you need strength, you need determination, you need pride, you need technique. . . . But even more important than these, you need love. And how I translate this is, that Cocteau is saying that the ultimate love of the artist is the gift of the work itself. When we present the work to the public. In this sense the act of communication itself is an act of generosity, of love; it's an act of connectedness. And so love in its most pure form is about relationship. In an artist's relationship with his or her audience this all comes into play. And I think that Cocteau was a *very* public artist.

CROWE: And what is the question in *Les enfants terribles*?
GLASS: By the time we get to *Les enfants*, both the question and the answer have become strangely twisted in a way. The focus becomes more the site of creativity, rather than the creative act itself. The metaphysics, if you will, of love becomes more concerned with the matter, the trapping of love, or creativity. In this story, it's the room that is the site of the interaction of the main characters. In *Orpheus*, it is the car that is "the site of love." The place where creativity, the creative act, is taking place. And in *La belle*, the site becomes the chateau.

CROWE: This is all very reminiscent of Bachelard. Bachelard's *The Poetics of Space*. Is there any indication, that you know of, that Cocteau may have gotten this idea of "space," of "poetic space" from Bachelard?
GLASS: I'm not sure, to tell you the truth. I don't know where Cocteau's idea may have originated. And I'm not familiar with this book you mention of Bachelard's, but I like the idea of "poetic space."

In terms of finding a metaphor for this site-related aspect of creativity, I refer to it as "the site of the intuitive." You could see, for instance, that the voyage of the father in *La belle et la bete* to the chateau, ultimately, is the journey of the artist into his own unconscious.

But, in *Les enfants terribles*, the site of creativity is the bedroom. So, in this story, the question becomes: "When and how can the site of creativity become liberating? And in which way can it become a prison?"

You see the appeal of Cocteau? I've never encountered anyone other than Cocteau who talks about the work this way. This idea of the artist's love affair with the work.

In *Les enfants*, the "love" of relationship and the "love" of creativity is clearly a narcissistic love. Here, it's not the love that is extended outward, but rather the love that turns inward. And as I say, the transformation occurring in this story is a narcissistic transformation, which ultimately ends in the self-destruction of both of the two central characters. And here Cocteau is, again, giving us guidelines about the path of the artist, and at the same time about relationships. In this case it's more about what an artist shouldn't do than what he should be doing. How self-indulgence of preoccupation can subvert the true creative process. How narcissism can undermine true love. . . . Here, this kind of preoccupation, instead of leading to transformation, leads to death.

So, of the three, *Orphee* is about transformation; *La belle et la bete* is a romantic opera, although dealing with the issue of transformation; and *Les Enfants* is a tragedy. It's a kind of cautionary tale in a way. It really picks up from *La Belle* and that which will transform this strange world we live in, then *Les enfants* is about what is missing in terms of the power of transformation. *Les enfants* is a kind of towering tragedy—reminiscent of Greek tragedy. The kind of thing where you're sitting there in your seat and watching this thing go on onstage and you want to jump up out of your seat and yell "no, no . . . stop, stop." But you can't stop it. It has to play out this way. The very seeds of the destruction were in the relationship itself, you see. When Cocteau says at the very beginning, "They were like two persons in one body," which is a very beautiful image on the one hand, he is already setting up the limitations of the relationship which won't allow for any kind of relationship to really develop or grow. All this duplicitous behavior is about the kind of unconsciousness that exists between the two characters. Largely due to their self-indulgent attitudes about themselves. They wouldn't know love if it hit them over the head, so to speak. Which is exactly what happens—with regard to their ignorance of even their own love for the other, much less the love of the other for them. Hence, the tragedy. And the final, tragic outcome.

NAN WATKINS: I want to ask you some questions that are pointed more toward the musical side of your collaborative process. The musical partnering with these literary librettos that goes hand in glove in your music-theater pieces. While you were with Nadia Boulanger in Paris in the early 1960s, I was in Vienna at the Academy of Music.
GLASS: Yes, you either went to Paris or you went to Vienna in those days.

WATKINS: I wonder if you could give a nutshell description of the legacy of Boulanger, and especially her influence on your work, both then and later.
GLASS: It's difficult to boil her down to just a nutshell, really, but the early formation of certain French influences was very much from her. It's no accident that my music sounds the way it does, and especially in the Cocteau pieces, as they all utilize the French language—the librettos are in French. Secondly, my teacher was a student of Fauré. In this sense the lineage is authentic and complete.

If I had to say simply one thing that I learned from her, I'd have to say that I learned the relationship between style and technique which, for me, was a very important lesson. And it was from her that I learned it. I learned, for example, that there is no such thing as "style," that is, unless it's based on technique. That technique without style simply cannot exist. It's like saying I want to be a poet—but I have no access to words or language of any kind. So, I was with her there in Paris for a couple of years, and before that, as I say, I studied with students of hers. It was only at the end of my studies that I began to realize what it was that she had taught me.

WATKINS: I'm very much interested in the ways in which you dissolve the lines between the pop and serious or classical music fields.

Between high art and low art. In that sense, could you tell us a little bit about how it is working with such "pop" musician/composers as Brian Eno and David Bowie, both of whom, one would have to say, are, like yourself, on the cutting edge of their respective fields of contemporary music.

GLASS: Sure, and that's very easy really, as I've known both of them as friends for well over twenty years.

David is a very intelligent man and very interested in art, and very easy to talk to. Not as musically sophisticated, in some ways, and yet he knows exactly what he wants to do musically. I have worked with David because of the musicality of his lyrics, essentially. The "naïve sophistication" of it. I really don't know any other way to say it.

Brian, on the other hand, is a very thoughtful man, who is extremely talented. I find his work inspiring, as I do David's, but in a different way.

Talking about music today . . . I was talking with Virgil Thompson some years ago. He had his ninetieth birthday the same year that I had my fiftieth and we were talking about opera. And as someone that I admired, who had come from a generation of operatic composers during a generation when there wasn't much to be admired in terms of what was being done in opera, he said to me: "Don't forget, Philip, opera is a public affair." And somehow I heard that, and understood what it was he meant. It's not enough for an artist to say, "I don't care what the public thinks." Especially someone who is working in a medium such as opera that is defined, really, by its audience.

But to get back to your question. . . . One of the interesting things about composers today, and not just Eno, Bowie, and myself, has to do with the primarily European idea that there is a high art culture and then there is a kind of public art culture. And that these two art cultures are, and in fact have to be, totally separate. Well, new or contemporary music composers will not tolerate that fact. Especially, I would say that this is true here in the United States.

How this figures in to people like me, is that I went out into the world of public performance as one of the people of my generation, along with a number of others, who made a point of that. Of not trying to separate the two worlds of influence. I go out into the world to find the sources for my music. I do sixty to seventy concerts a year, and I talk continuously about these kinds of things to people like yourself. So, the idea here that I'm trying to get across is that we are making ourselves available, and the work accessible. We want our work to be part of contemporary culture, not focusing on a culture that is relegated to a handful of specially educated people.

As a young man, during the 1960s, myself and my friends were very interested in people like Jasper Johns, Andy Warhol, in poetry, in writing, in theater. . . . But when it came to music, my friends only wanted to listen to rock-and-roll. And I began asking myself: "What is going on here? Why isn't contemporary music taking its place in the world as a part of contemporary culture?" My friends liked films, they liked plays, and they liked poetry . . . but they would only listen to rock-and-roll. What was going on here, I kept asking myself. I mean, Allen Ginsberg was out giving readings and public performances all the time! And not only just Ginsberg, but Corso and some of the others. . . . Meanwhile, all the composers at the time were giving little concerts in little recital halls, with charts and explanations so that people could follow them. What I'm trying to say here is that there was something wrong with this picture.

So, some of the members of my generation decided, and we were determined, to initiate a dialogue with the public, while the older generation was not concerned about the public at all. To compose with the public in mind was considered to be some kind of unacceptable compromise of their work. You see the whole thing was kind of precious, or so intellectual that one could even, in that sense, say elite. Meanwhile, composers of serious music were losing their audience. In this case, to rock-and-roll.

[*At this point in the conversation, which was going on outside in the courtyard of Glass's hotel where we were sitting and*

talking around a small umbrella-covered table, we were inter-
rupted by a "parade" of employees pushing large utility carts on
wheels across a long cobblestone walkway—making an unusual
if not unruly noise. Just at the moment that the noise came close
enough to get his attention and to cause him to lose his train of
thought, Glass quickly smiled, and with a kind of devilish twin-
kle in his eye, turned to look at the caravan of carts, then turned
back with a wide grin and said: "A Cage piece!" All of us broke
into laughter.]

What I'm trying to say here is that for me, for us, dialogue was
one of the most essential aspects of the composition of new music.
But for the older generation of composers, it was probably the least
important factor. For me, the dialogue existed on the highest end
of the curve. So, I was concerned with the question of what it was
that was going to make it possible to have a world in which such a
dialogue could exist.

I'm happy to report that in just a very short time—in just twen-
ty-five short years—that that reality that we were dreaming of in
the sixties, has, in fact, become a reality. And now composers of
modern music are "out there," on the road, playing their music to
audiences of all kinds. I suppose that there will always be a contin-
gent of academics in any and all the art forms—and that's all right
with me, but it's not my style or my path.

In fact, I was just recently in Florida at a large conference for
composers, and we were talking about just this very thing. There
were about thirty or forty composers from the different schools,
and they were of a consensus that this more public position, this
attitude embracing a true dialogue with the audience, was not only
admirable, but necessary. They said that in the past they wouldn't
have been willing to admit to this change of heart, but that now
they were. And they liked the idea that the music was going out
beyond the ivory-towered-and-clad walls of academia.

WATKINS: One could say that to take that more conservative, aca-
demic position these days is pretty much a dead end.

GLASS: It's completely a dead end! As a young man, I very early came to the conclusion that I was not going to spend the rest of my life writing my music for sixty people. I was looking for something quite different from that.

And to get back to Cocteau—he certainly would have understood, as did Virgil Thompson, this more modern sentiment. In fact, Cocteau was so attracted to film *because* it was such a public art form. Cocteau was never one to stand in awe or in fear of the public—or to be in the public eye, for that matter. Fear of the public is something that my generation had to overcome. We had inherited it, in some ways, from the previous generation. And what this dilemma, and the overcoming of this pubic fear, led us to was essentially the reform of the language of modern music. Nothing short of that. It was, you could say, a wholesale, direct attack on the institutions and techniques of modern music that had come down to us at the beginning of the second half of the century; and we were looking at a complete new form of language. And after a time, people began taking seriously the notion that that was, and is, exactly what we are doing. The academics in those early years thought that we were clowns. But who's laughing now?! [Laughs.]

WATKINS: To get back on the subject of collaboration . . . Another modern music composer who has recently worked and collaborated with David Bowie is a talented young turk named Trent Reznor— the founder of the alternative rock group called Nine Inch Nails. Having seen a recent performance of Reznor and his band, I was struck how the performance was nothing short of what Wagner referred to as a "Gesamtkunstwerk." Very Wagnerian—utilizing every theatrical device imaginable, and in grand style. I'm wondering if you are familiar with Reznor, or have seen the sort of performance he puts on—very much a cathartic, audience-oriented event.

GLASS: No, I haven't, but I'd like to see that. It sounds very much like what it is that I do!

WATKINS: Yes, exactly. But what I was particularly struck by was the overall cathartic effect of Reznor's music. After two and a half hours of high-intensity and high-decibel music, the effect on the audience was almost calming. I'm wondering if, in your process of composing and producing your music and operas, if you are purposefully intent on achieving a desired effect upon your audiences.

GLASS: Yes, we, and I have to use the word "we," since I am almost always working in tandem with other artists, are always working toward some sort of catharsis with an audience in mind. As I said earlier, the audience aspect of any composition and performance is equal if not foremost in our mind.

Again, this all goes back to Cocteau—and his preoccupation with the transformative power of art. Transforming the ordinary world of experiences into an extra-ordinary world. This, in fact, is not something that only artists do, but something that everyone does. If you buy a vase of flowers and put them on the kitchen table, you're basically transforming your kitchen. Whether we are conscious of it or not, we all are tirelessly and continuously going about the business of transforming our world. We are always doing that. What sets the artist apart from other people, in this regard, is that he has made this everyday process his profession.

WATKINS: You would seem—judging from your output, the volume of work alone—to be very comfortable with making this process your profession. And to accomplish all that you have over the years, one would have to, I think, be very professional and businesslike in the process.

GLASS: Yes, and one of the things that continues to interest me about the activity of the artist, is that the whole experience I find to be one that is extremely positive. In fact, there are almost no negatives to it, in my experience. One couldn't honestly say this, I don't think, about lawyers, politicians, or military people and their jobs.

The artist's work, like that of the healer or the teacher—what we have in common is that both the motivation and the effects of the art form are (or should be) entirely positive. The question becomes: What can I do that will be totally beneficial to both other people and to myself at the same time? Both this question and its answer should be the proper motivation for the healer, the teacher, and the artist. And by artist I mean the poet, the painter, the playwright, the musician, the dancer . . . all these. We talk about these professions as being vocations, as being "callings." Not as being professions in the same sense as those of the engineer or the doctor (at least doctors as we know them today). For these "called" professions, it's not about money, or the making of money. It's about the process. The beneficial effect that their work will have on their "audience." The same thing that I'm sure Wagner, and your Trent Reznor set out to achieve. The artist shouldn't be surprised by his audience experiencing catharsis. So, in this sense, intent and motivation is everything.

Is this catharsis something that is temporary, or is it, rather, something that truly changes your world? The answer to whether or not it is just the temporary high has to do with the quality of the work. So the question becomes just how deeply the powers of transformation are operative.

WATKINS: One final question to try and tie this all together. . . . Since we began with the question of Boulanger and your "nutshell" response to that part of your life, I'd like to ask where you find yourself today with regard to composition and the kind of music you are composing currently as compared with, say, your early work. What has, or does, define those differences? Has there been a major development over the arc of your personal and professional history?

GLASS: Again, in a "nutshell," as you say, the happiest development has been my ability to collaborate with other artists. This is something that I have learned to do over the years. [Looking at and making an aside to Thomas Crowe] This is probably not something that I would have said to you in 1990, right?

CROWE: Not that I remember.

GLASS: What has grown over the years is my appetite for collaboration and, as well, I think, even my skills at knowing how to bring people together. This includes knowing how to give ample room to someone in order that they can do their work. Knowing how to delegate certain areas of work to other people. Knowing how *not* to be a control freak and a tyrant. To allow any kind of collaborative partnership to be a joyful experience, for all concerned. To allow even the possibility of love to become part of that experience. This means being vulnerable. Being willing to be flexible with your ideas—maybe even giving up your ideas in order to let the other person work to their capacity, or to explore their own ideas. Do you see what I mean? Two words come to mind, here: "synthesis" and "synergy." In fact, the synergy of artists coming together is so much greater than the ideas, the images, or the visions that I bring individually into a piece. The truth of the matter is, that I am dependent upon the talents of other artists to do what I do. The fact of this demands that I have learned, over the years, the skills of cooperation.

WATKINS: And what about the composing itself? How has the process of making music changed for you over the years, if at all?

GLASS: Let me respond to that by saying that I've found that the first problem of any composer is to find a "voice," and the second problem is to get rid of it. The burden of identity can be overwhelming, at a certain point. And the biggest struggle we have is to get rid of it. One of the things about collaboration is that it is a great antidote to self-absorption. Something that a closely defined style demands and encourages.

With each collaborative piece I work on I work with a different dynamic of people, of artists. This demands that my working process and my ideas about my own music change in accordance with the demands of each given situation. So, in this way, my approaches to composition you could say are constantly changing. Changing with each new performance piece I undertake. Each piece requires a different recipe, and that recipe requires, in turn, different ingredients—or in this case, a different kind of music. In fact, I depend on my collaborators to get me out of the rut of the self. To relieve me from the burden of having to be myself on a day-to-day basis. To help me "transform," to use again Cocteau's term, my working reality. And to make it a positive one.

EUGENE FRIESEN

More Than the Music

Eugene Friesen was born in 1952, the son of Mennonite parents who immigrated from Russia as children. He began cello studies in elementary school at the urging of his father, a church musician and conductor, and participated in his father's choral and orchestral productions of major sacred works from the age of twelve. The use of symphonic instruments in the pop music of the 1960s was another influence. This duality remained strong throughout Friesen's college years, when he played both in a jazz-rock band, The Modern Fur-Bearing Orchestra, and the Fresno Philharmonic.

It was in Fresno, in 1973, that Eugene first met Paul Winter at one of Winter's music workshops. So impressed was Winter with this young cellist that five years later Friesen, by then a graduate of the Yale School of Music, was invited to join the Consort. As a member of the Paul Winter Consort since 1978, Eugene's gift for the responsive flow of improvised music has been featured in concerts throughout Europe, Japan, Brazil, the United States, and Canada.

Since then, Eugene has toured with the Consort, as well as with Trio Globo, also featuring Howard Levy and Glen Velez. His credits as a composer include three television scores aired on PBS and a collaboration with Richard Peaslee on the Obie award–winning score for *The Garden of Earthly Delights*. Eugene's *Earth Requiem: Stories of Hope* had its 1991 premiere at Southern Connecticut State University, and *Grasslands*, a major piece for the Paul Winter Consort, orchestra, and choir, was premiered in Kansas in June 1997.

Eugene has performed and recorded with the Paul Winter Consort, with whom he won a Grammy award in 1994 and 1995. With Trio Globo, he has been featured in concerts all over the world with such diverse artists as Dave Brubeck, Toots Thielemans, Yevgeny Yevtushenko, Coleman Barks, Betty Buckley, Anthony Davis, and Scott Cossu. He has performed as a soloist at the International Cello Festival in Manchester, England; Rencontres d'Ensembles de Violoncelles in Beauvais, France; and at the World Cello Congress in Baltimore, Maryland.

His compositional credits include four albums of original music: *In the Shade of Angels*, *New Friend*, *Arms Around You*, and *The Song of Rivers*; and two collaborative albums: *The Bremen Town Musicians* with Bob Hoskins and *Sabbaths* with poems by Wendell Berry, and a new CD *Pure Water* with Rumi poems translated and read by Coleman Barks. He has also done numerous scores for documentary films.

Eugene Friesen is on the faculty of the Berklee College of Music in Boston. He lives in Vermont with his wife, Wendy, and children. Considered a breakthrough artist by many, Paul Winter has said of Eugene Friesen's music: "Thanks to Eugene Friesen, one of the most sexy and soulful instruments in the world has been liberated!" A man who is quite literally married to his music, Eugene Friesen is a very comfortable combination of the thoughtful and the spontaneous. A man who is both the contemplative and lamenting personification of the songs from his first solo album *New Friend*, as well as the joyous and celebratory man reflected in the mirror of his newer releases. And quite frankly, Eugene Friesen is one of the most passionate solo performers I have ever witnessed. The interaction between this man and his instrument is comparable to nothing less than the sensuous dance of embracing lovers. And the sounds that are the result of this caressive style of playing are the correspondence of the mutually sworn vows of that love.

Also a lover of life, Friesen is an active environmentalist, a self-styled philosopher, a world traveler, and a whimsical prankster. In 1989, Eugene had become one of North Carolina's most visible, if not applauded, new residents. I had seem him in concert with the Paul Winter Consort on several occasions and even written a lengthy review of one of those performances. But when I met him in 1990, it was serendipitous, as we were both on the program as part of an event sponsored and put together by Howard Hanger and the Howard Hanger Jazz Fantasy in Asheville, North Carolina. The poetry and music we both had selected that evening seemed to be so compatible that we both were inspired to speak to the other about the possibility of working together in a more intentionally collaborative way.

During the three or more years that followed, we collaborated for several poetry and music performances, which included performances with pianist/composer Paul Sullivan as well as a gala event in Detroit in 1991 with other members of the Winter Consort (Paul Halley and Glen Velez). These performances culminated with the production and release of a live performance recording entitled *The Sound of Light*, which was produced and distributed by Holocene Press, and which is now a product of Fern Hill Records.

Having the geographic good fortune in those days to be within shouting distance of his home, during one of my visits to his farmhouse high in the hills of the Sugar Grove community in western North Carolina, we spent a late fall afternoon pruning apple trees, slopping the hogs, and talking about some of the deeper issues that lay beneath the obvious in his music, in his memory, and in his dreams.

THOMAS RAIN CROWE: Let's begin at the beginning. Could you give me a general sketch of your personal and musical background and those things that have been "building blocks" for who you are and what you are doing?

EUGENE FRIESEN: I was raised in the suburbs of California. My parents were Mennonite—immigrants from the Russian Mennonite communities who migrated to Canada as children. They eventually made their way down into the U.S. and Kansas, and, finally, to southern California. So the Mennonite Church was a vital part of my upbringing. And I had my first musical experiences there.

My father was a musician and a choral conductor until the age of about eighty. He was an obvious influence early on as was the musical training in the public schools until I began with private musical study as a teenager—which I suppose some would consider as starting relatively late. It was only as a college student that I really decided to commit to the music in a serious sense.

Early, growing up in the 1960s, American pop music was my biggest source of influence and inspiration. Later, my search was for a new cultural context for the cello, which I had by this time taken as my seminal vehicle for musical expression. I was a student of classical music in a sense, but when I was in high school I began writing songs that were a combination of folk and pop. My first band was a thirteen-piece rock band. It had a cello, violin, viola, two trumpets, baritone sax, drums, bass, organ, guitars, and, of course, a lead-singer. And I did the writing for that group. I stayed with this group and this outlet for my musical expression until about the age of twenty-three, at which time I started to focus single-mindedly on the cello, to go deeper into the study of this instrument, and to fill out my education, which up to that point had been largely self-inflicted. So, I got "heavy into" the cello I guess you could say. Practicing between five and twelve hours a day. And ended up going to the Yale School of Music where I eventually received the equivalent of a degree which they called a "Certificate of Performance." This was a special program, so technically I did not receive your classic undergraduate degree, but the Certificate was more to the point of the direction I wanted to go in with my work with the cello.

When I got out of Yale, I started performing with Paul Winter. I had met Paul in 1973, we did some improvising, and he took my name down and five years later he gave me a call. So we're up to 1978 when the first serious collaborative work with the Consort began for me.

Two years later, in 1980, I began working, also, with the Delos String Quartet. This group was mostly a European touring quartet with which I did, I think, six European tours. We had won an international competition for string quartets in France when two years later (1982) I decided to leave this group and devote myself full-time to the work of the Consort. Which brings us up pretty much to the present and my focus of developing new music for the cello, which includes work with theatre groups, with dancers, choral groups, and now, of all things, with poets! [Laughs.]

CROWE: How has your experience with the Paul Winter Consort affected your more recent musical tastes and interests?

FRIESEN: Many of the musicians who have played with the Consort have kind of tongue-in-cheek referred to it as the "Paul Winter Graduate School of Music." This affiliation has been extremely positive for me in several ways. First, I suppose, would be learning the role of leadership. Leadership as a "group leader" whose primary priorities are focused on service. By service I mean serving the people who come to listen and participate in the music performed.

Secondly, the experiences of nature have profoundly effected both my thinking and my playing. When I started playing with the Consort I doubt that I had ever been camping and so, therefore, was a real "house peasant" in the Western sense. Not at all comfortable with nature. Not at all experienced with being out of doors. So to go down to the Bay of Magdalena to meet with the grey whales, for example, truly opened up a whole new world for me; a world of divinity. That one experience eye to eye with the grey whales showed me the spiritual and the divine aspects of life, and my worldview, consequently, expanded dramatically! Likewise, what I experienced after three weeks of rafting down the Colorado River in the Grand Canyon searching for resident places for taping music based on our experiences and findings there, was another real opening experience for me. Just the fact of being outside, constantly, for three weeks, which I had never done, became a real initiation. Being in this deep rock canyon and feeling the vibrations, the sounds of this place, the presences of the "ancient ones"—the Anasazi—enlarged my sense of being and, in fact, initiated my interest in Native American cultures and traditions which has become more and more an influence on my thinking and in my music.

So, in these ways, as well as having the opportunities to play our own music—to have a vehicle in place to perform that music which we've written—has also been very important to me in terms of my growth as a composer. Also, I should add: the opportunities to improvise—opportunities such as being flung out onstage with no other introduction or instruction except "OK, it's time to do a cello solo," and to just spontaneously play. To play by heart. By "by heart" I don't mean "playing by memory" which is what many people think of as playing by heart. What I'm referring to is playing from this creative place where you don't know with your mind what's going to happen next. And that's the kind of situation, the kind of risk-taking, which sometimes allows you to tap this great creative wellspring of music which, when released, flows forth. Playing *from* the heart . . .

This improvising, I realized, was very much like life. We're always having to "wing it," to improvise continuously each day as we're thrown up against new and unplanned circumstances; and I believe that it's our intrinsic creativity in these situations that really gets us through.

Perhaps a final thing about the Consort, with regards to your question of effects and/or influences, would be the extraordinary human experience I have had. The warm and very human sense of community that working with the members of the Consort has afforded me. In addition to the group itself, I have found it very heartening that almost everywhere we play there is a small core group of people who are sympathetic to the issues surrounding the Consort's music: issues having to do with the environment, endangered species, or some ecologically related topic. This makes the touring so much richer than simply the act of walking out onstage night after night and plucking strings. After many years now of traveling and performing, it's more like visiting extended family in these places all over this country and the world than simply putting on a show.

CROWE: Speaking of "extended family" and community, I'm curious as to how your work with the Consort and all this traveling over the years has affected you—has maybe even changed you and the way you perceive yourself now as being a part of the world around you.

FRIESEN: I began playing with the Consort, as I said, right out of music school. And in music school I was completely devoted to my art, my craft; and of course, my focus was on playing the cello. Playing the traditional masterpieces of music. In that respect it's a tradition that has its feet in a previous century. Even music written in this century harkens back to a sensibility of a previous century. Coming out of that and into the context of my work with the Consort—immediately I found myself in a music-making situation which was focused on the reality of the time that we are, *now*, living in. This music-making with the Consort was not music-for-the-sake-of-music alone or for purposes of *self* expression, but it was music that was coming from people in a "family." In a large family. People who are connected as a family to the Earth itself. And as a member of that bigger family, we are talking about things that were of concern, in a celebrational sense, to the whole family which inhabits what we were calling "the global village." In that respect, this experience was a radical about-face for me. To turn from the classical music situation of presenting music by other composers from past times and breathing new life into it from my own personal point of view, to actually *creating* music, participating in a music which spoke to things that were urgent to the moment they were played. It was kind of a shift from being a *performer* of music to an active *creator* of music. And the assumption is: that the creator of music creates music that is happening, through this creative process, to the planet at any given time. That's part of "a healing wave" that affects the planet and is part of the solution, just as problems are arising at the same time.

The result of this kind of focus coming from the influences of the Consort has meant speaking a different language musically for me, as well. Even though the music that I was playing previously has its roots in the various traditions of Western music, I've found that because our habits of music-listening have changed (primarily as the result of the ways in which we are constantly surrounded by different forms of the media) the musical vocabulary that really speaks to people, that can really communicate with the common person, is a kind of music that is more accessible. For me, someone who was coming out of music school, it was also a much simpler music that I found myself playing with the Consort. And quite honestly I didn't respect myself for it, initially, because it seemed too easy to play. I perceived myself as communicating with my new audiences in a "cheaper" way somehow—because I wasn't using all the many skills that I was over-prepared with as a result of my time at music school. So, it was really a shift in coming to a political awareness of the present time from being in that "art-for-art's-sake" realm of music-making where I was developing all the various "musical tools" with which to dazzle audiences into a lullaby of the past.

CROWE: If I am hearing you correctly, are you saying, then, that your work with the Winter Consort has instilled in you a greater sense or awareness of yourself as being in the present? The "Be Here Now" idea, for example, that is associated so often with Ram Dass and the 1960s.

FRIESEN: That's certainly something that is important to me—the notion of being here *now*—but I have to confess right off that this is something I'm not good at, in practice. In fact, I suspect that one of the reasons why I am as drawn to music-making as I am is because I think it is the thing I engage in which draws me most into the present. I feel the most present when I am making music. But in general the whole process of maturing for me has been a process of coming into the presence of the present time. And I've found that it takes a lot of courage to do that because it forces me to admit to real things, which are often unpleasant, that are going on. And it is, of course, much easier to deny those things. And I've traveled that path, too, and for a long time. But the thing that comes along with admitting and really seeing things by coming into the present is this rush of energy, color, and vibration—vibrancy! This is the payoff side of the process.

More to the point, you were inferring about "place" or "home." I have this real thing about the notion of "home." The music that seems to touch me the deepest somehow speaks to me of "home." And by "home" I don't mean a home that I have had before, but rather some "other" kind of home. The word that the Brazilians have for this is: *saudade*. It connotes a nostalgia for a home you've never had. I experience this sense of saudade when I am witness to an exquisite sunset, hear a wonderful piece of music, or see an unearthly beautiful woman. Even an act of humility or an act of forgiveness can make me nostalgic for this place called "home."

CROWE: So, how does being on the road as much as you are effect your actually *being* in a place, as well as your profound *sense* of or feeling for that place?

FRIESEN: First of all, I feel very fortunate that I haven't ever toured with a mainstream "successful" group such as a big-name rock band. From what I know of those kinds of tours, they can be extremely impersonal—playing huge halls for huge audiences. Consequently, these performers never really get a sense of the identity of the audience. And in fact it seems that in order to attract an audience of that size, what you are playing for that audience has to have a diminished sense of individuality and character to it. As to the touring done with the Consort, very often we are promoted by very specific local groups. For example, perhaps a Wolf Preservation organization, or a Whale Research outfit will bring us into a place to perform. So, in general our audiences are small (1,000–2,000 people), and because of that, or one of the things that happens because of that, we get to meet people from the audience. Through our direct interaction with our audiences we get the feeling, at least, of what that specific locale has to offer. Over the years from this kind of touring we've made friends in various places who give me a sense, when I'm in these places, of what's going on or what issues are important there. These regions have a particular, unique character that helps to define them and that helps me to experience myself in a nurturing sort of way while there.

CROWE: Much of the message of the Consort's music seems to have its roots imbedded deep in the ideas of "celebrating our diversity," "extended family," and acceptance in the form of "re-inhabitation." Where, and on what kind of scale have you seen these ideas being acted out, globally, in human communities?

FRIESEN: Those are things that transcend the bioregional thing. Those are things common to every (bio)region. Things that are metaphoric to Nature itself. This country [the United States] is the place that seems to have spawned these ideas for everywhere else. And there may be interesting surmisals to make as to why that is. Maybe there is some quality indigenous to this land itself that somehow brings about the consciousness, the actions, toward the land. This sense of the sacredness of the land. And the consequential role of stewards that we have with it. But I have definitely seen this in other places, as well. In places as unlikely as the former Soviet Union, where people were suffering under the weight of an enormous (if now fragmented) monolithic state—an inefficient overpowering bureaucracy. Even there I saw signs of hope. Signs of people becoming involved with local environmental issues.

Another place where the consciousness toward the environment is growing in leaps and bounds is Japan. When the Japanese do things they do them in an amazingly conscientious way. They are losing some of their natural habitat and some of their natural places. Once they develop as a priority the preservation of those places, they will become fanatically involved with it. And because they are more or less "on top of the heap" economically, I think we will see these kinds of environmental priorities trickle down to other economies as well. But you see it in Brazil, too, where the theme of a recent year's Carnival was "Honoring the Environment of the Earth." Here the "Samba Schools" (community music and dance organizations) were active in making floats and displays embellishing sub-themes around this central Carnival theme having to do with the preservation of those-things-natural.

I've seen evidence of this type of awareness and activism in all the countries I've visited. But one never knows if that growth in awareness is happening on levels consistent with the level of destruction or inattention! But I *can* say that there *are* signs of hope for those who are concerned.

CROWE: What, would you say, then, is the motivating ideology or vision behind what the Consort is doing?
FRIESEN: I think I can answer that. I know, for instance, that Paul sees himself as an educator to a large extent. And, of course, his gift, his educational vehicle, is music. He has a very clear sense of how powerfully music communicates. I would say that with Paul, his great passion is to communicate. And he wants to talk about the things he's most concerned about in these times in which we are living. For him that means these creatures—the whale, the wolf, the eagle. . . . His experiences of time spent in communion, in direct communication, with these creatures results in his falling in love with them. I think quite literally. And it is "beauty" that ties all of us in the group together. It's both the "lure" and the "bonding element" that makes the Consort and its music what it is. And here, again, we're back to that connection with divinity, this time as the result of beauty, in all its forms.

CROWE: As a cellist, with the cello being almost universally considered to be a classical instrument, how do you see yourself working to bridge the gap between popular music audiences and those who predominantly support classical music? Is there, do you think, a middle or common ground?
FRIESEN: It's a struggle to get past that initial hesitation that people have with something like the cello. But this hesitation, I've found, is primarily intellectual, as I've been amazed with the numbers of people who come up to me after a concert and exclaim, "Oh, the cello, that's my favorite instrument!" And yet, you're right, most people know it as something which belongs on the right-hand side of the stage in a symphony concert hall. Not that many people have heard a cello by itself, but when they do I've found that they experience it as being a very *human* instrument. As to how to lug this

big thing across that "bridge" . . . well, I think it's the *rhythm*. The cello is, traditionally, a very lyric instrument. It's an instrument that plays a sad or noble melody. There's something in the makeup of the instrument itself that emits a lamenting quality. Yet, the things that I've had great fun with and have been able to surprise people with is playing it very rhythmically. Playing it rhythmically to the point that people have actually become concerned about my instrument. Concerned for its safety. Sometimes they will even ask me, "Is your cello all right!?" And although I never do anything while performing to actually injure the instrument, sometimes the sharp accents and cross-rhythms and other various effects that occur while improvising, apparently would, to those listening and watching, seem to indicate to them that my instrument is crying out in various forms of pain! [Laughs.] And so I console them by assuring them that this isn't so. Yes, in response to your question, it is the *rhythm* that is really the "bridge-maker."

Yet, there is, perhaps, one other element that I would add here in response to your question, and this is, as is evident on my CD *Arms Around You*, the added depth and sound that is brought to the instrument in the company of other instruments and players. On this particular CD, the full rhythm section (which includes four or five percussionists) adds influences from Latin America, Africa, and from American jazz. With these added influences and the added dimension to the overall sound, there are more familiar factors available for the audience to recognize and identify with.

But probably the clincher—that factor that most powerfully brings the cello back "home" to the listener—is its similarity to the human voice. It has been said by musicologists that the cello is the closest instrument in approximation to the human voice. And it is because of this similarity that the cello can and does touch people very deeply. And when coupled with the human voice, the union makes for a beautiful blending—and in the ears and eyes of the audience the cello, then, becomes a little more viable as a solo instrument in a band.

CROWE: I want to talk a little about your CD *Arms Around You*. I want to know about it in terms of its sense of freshness for you. I also want to know how contemporary it feels to you in terms of it being in sync with the current directions in which cutting-edge contemporary music is heading.

FRIESEN: The music on *Arms Around You*, in general, is less intimate than my first album, *New Friend*, which was done almost as a duet (myself and keyboard artist John Halley) in the Cathedral of St. John the Divine in New York City. An album which comes off, I feel, very personal because of its simplicity and its intimate interaction of cello and piano or cello and organ. The second album *Arms Around You*, by contrast, is comprised of original compositions designed for a large ensemble. We did a lot of experimenting to find the ensemble that would best support this sound of the cello. In a very literal sense we were designing the vehicle that could carry this thing, this idea, off. In addition to these pieces there are also two improvisational pieces, which are similar to how the first album was conceived and created.

In *Arms Around You* my compositions seem to create a "bridge" as you say, but as well to feature the cello as a solo instrument with a capacity for great joy. This album is a very "songful" album, very melodic, and is, I think, very joyous. This joyousness is achieved not only through an up-tempo playing style of the cello, but as a result of a driving rhythm section which incorporates extensive use of percussive instruments. And because of these changes and the differences from the first album, I think it is a much more accessible album.

There was much work to do that had never been done before to make the cello work as a strong feasible solo instrument. And, yes, this new album has granted me a much greater sense of being present and being contemporary with current newnesses that seem to be infiltrating the consciousness of modern music and modern musicians.

CROWE: Having worked our way up through your musical past to the present, where, then, do you see—where would you like to see—your music going both with and without the Consort in the not-too-distant future?

FRIESEN: My first two CDs I see as a way of establishing the voice of the cello. They really concentrate on the cello, itself, attempting to make it a viable and respected voice. From here on out, I think that I'll continue to enjoy the cello as a solo instrument, but my aim is to continue to compose music that communicates the ideals and the vision of a sustainable future, environmentally. This idea is related directly to a pet project of mine that I am calling "Grasslands," a project that focuses on the midwestern grasslands region centered primarily in and around the state of Kansas. The region so eloquently written about by agricultural activist Wes Jackson. I've made several visits to the region, read and studied up on it wherever I could find available resource materials. I'm interested in this region's ecological history as well as its most distant recorded human history. What I've done with the grasslands concept is to internationalize it in scale by comparing similar habitats and ecosystems on other continents, such as Africa and Asia, and to document the potential health and sustainability of these areas toward creating a musical model of sorts to hold up in the face of the kinds of devastation and erosion we are seeing now in the grasslands here in this country. The "history of the life of the prairie," I guess you could summarize, and the effects of human habitation on this kind of environment.

I can hear music, for example, that would include African instruments similar to those used by the grassland tribes in Africa with their incredible rhythms. Musical statements coming also from the traditional cultures in the Americas, as well. In this sense, the buffalo would be one of the players in this musical drama, also the wind, and the big sky. In this "big band prairie sound" a true emphasis would come from the various percussive influences of these indigenous cultures. This, mixed with the modern use of cello and choral counterpoint to create a musical form that, much as jazz is to this country as an indigenous musical creation, would be reflective of a global musical style that is a true reflection of the natural world and all its "songs."

CROWE: I'm curious as to your musical interests. Interests perhaps outside of your obvious interests with regard to the cello and its rich tradition. What kinds of new or even old music excites you at this point in your life and career?

FRIESEN: I guess what excites me most are great performances of any kind. Aside from the real thing, live, right now the CD I am listening to the most is an anthology of recordings made in the fields and on the plains of Africa by various tribes. These tracks are predominantly vocal with some percussive background—gourds, shakers, etc.—with little children doing antiphonal chanting.

In general, the music that seems to excite me is the music that grows out of a specific place, from a specific tradition. On a personal note, I almost long to be part of that kind of tradition, but I'm not. I perceive myself as a rootless person. There's no particular piece of ground that I can relate to and spring out of, with a music that is really indigenous to that place. I have embraced in my short lifetime the musical history and the culture of Western civilization—and it is from these traditions that my music has evolved. Even though my musical vocabulary is specifically Western, it is the result of my excitement on hearing music from these non-Western indigenous traditional cultures that have influenced my improvising.

Ironic, you might say, that the kinds of music that turn me on the most are those kinds of music that are rapidly being lost. The music of indigenous peoples everywhere. But, I must admit, I do enjoy listening to classical music and to those who I consider "the master musicians," which certainly includes the great jazz musicians.

In general, it is music that is melodic and that communicates something greater than just the idiom from whence it comes, that truly interests and excites me. So, it is not just "great jazz" that excites me, it is when great jazz becomes a great statement, a great communication that transcends the medium of jazz that really does it for me.

CROWE: You have done quite a bit of collaborative, interdisciplinary work with artists in other creative fields. How do you feel that that kind of creative interaction has benefited you?

FRIESEN: It's the stimulation, first of all. It's being able to transcend your own expectations. The ability to pull yourself out of the various traps that you weave around yourself. Escaping from those "safe cocoons." But the biggest advantage I've found coming from this process of working with other artists from different disciplines from my own is just to know, or at least begin to become aware of, when we are *truly* communicating. With the kind of intimate distance this kind of process gives us—in pursuit of an "intoxicating novelty"—these kinds of openings are made available for us and for a moment, if we're lucky and if we're quick, we can *see*.

CROWE: What, then, specifically, are some of the projects that you are currently working on both with the Winter group and with regard to your solo career?
FRIESEN: There are a number of things, actually. There are two things specifically that the Consort is up to with regard to new music. One is an album centered around the idea of "The Tree," which is an album related to the rainforest issue. The concept, however, for the album as it stands at present will be a dovetailing of this rainforest issue with the timing and significance of the winter solstice. Here, musically, we will be tapping into the native cultures of South America in particular and attempting to work with the rhythms of those traditions as well as celebrating the Festival of Light in relation to the solstice. But the main focus here is the issue surrounding man's use and misuse of the tree communities around the world and the repercussions that has on all life on the planet.

The other project is focused on the area of Lake Baikal in southern Siberia near the Mongolian border. Lake Baikal contains 22 percent of the world's fresh water and is comparable in size to the Grand Canyon. It is about 350 miles long, a mile deep, and up to 85 miles wide in some places—an awesome, huge, pure lake. A lake that is referred to by Russians as the Sacred Sea. We are planning to make several trips to Baikal in tandem with our concert trips and touring in that part of the world. There are many things that are unique to this lake region, one of which is that it is the home of the world's only freshwater seal, which for Paul is an attraction enough itself. Also, in terms of botanical considerations, there is a huge diversity of plant species as well as plants indigenous to and only found around the lake. Given our love for Russian vocal music as evidenced by our album *Earthbeat*, this project is very close to our hearts.

CROWE: And what about your own work separate from that with the Consort?

FRIESEN: The thing that is at the top of the list for me at present is the establishing of a touring ensemble—for live performances. This idea is very exciting to me as I am a performer at heart. I've *got* to be out there onstage. One of the aspects of this project that is exciting to me is the process of selection and of the evolving membership of the ensemble itself. For example, Glen Velez, the shamanistic percussionist who also plays with the Consort and who is a master of international drum styles, brings a special aspect to any group of musicians he performs with. And it is this kind of "specialness" that I am both looking for and excited by in terms of the formation of this new touring group. Yes, I'd say that almost all my focused energies with regard to my own solo work are going into this venture. Along with my composing, this idea of a "dream band" is foremost on my mind a good bit of the time, and the process of seeing this beginning to come together is exciting.

CROWE: I'm interested in your sense of yourself as a musician. By this I mean, what do you perceive as being "the role of the musician"? What are the musician's obligations to his or her self, first of all, and secondly, to the community around him or her locally or globally depending upon one's particular scale of vision?

FRIESEN: Part of who I am as a musician carries with it a desire to serve, through music. However, I have also found in my musical work that my intentions don't always play an important part. As a composer and as an improviser I've found that in my intentional work as a creator of music, as a composer, the music that is manifest in that way falls far short in communication, power, and vibrancy in comparison to the music that comes out through a good improvisation. Consequently, much of my composed work sits now in large piles of manuscript paper and notebooks.

I've found that through improvising, when a good improvisation happens, that I don't feel like it is me doing the improvising. It feels, rather, like it is happening *to* me. In that way I feel very present and very relaxed in knowing that the music that is coming out is the result of my relationship with the cello, which includes my technique and my body-balance on the instrument and the things that I am comfortable transmitting in that way, emotionally and psychically.

CROWE: Can we talk "shop" a little, here? Talk to me about getting work out to people. About supply and demand.

FRIESEN: Most people in our culture have been taught to think that musical entertainment is a commodity that they are in need of. So, the first and most obvious method of distribution would be as entertainment. Other kinds of supply and demand would include engaging in music as a way of reducing stress. There is a high demand for more meditative music, it seems, these days. Another way, and a way which is probably more appropriate for me, is as a way of observing nature. Of really participating in nature. There is a lot of "information" that one's soul yearns for, I believe. Listening to music can provide one with some of this information, education.

For me, justice toward the Earth is a question of self-education. Of being aware of what happens where. Because of this conscious position I have arrived at, I am on just about every mailing list imaginable—asking for donations. As dehumanizing as this process can be, I have realized that for myself this is a way in which I can affect things. By sending money to organizations I feel deeply about. So I do that. In a sense this is my "tithing." Instead of the church, I am giving to environmental groups, animal rights groups, etc. This, too, is part of your supply and demand paradigm.

CROWE: Let's talk about humor. Particularly humor in relation to music. The cello would seem to be a fairly "serious" instrument—one that would seem to an outsider to make certain serious demands upon its player. If this is true, do you see yourself, then, as a serious person as a result of your long-term relationship with the cello?

FRIESEN: We Americans express our humor much differently than other cultures. In classical music the humor is expressed in a very refined way. And if you're tuned in to the language and the musical customs of the time, you can then begin to appreciate the unexpected and the humor in that music—from Mozart and Haydn, in particular, which contains much great levity. The best way I can think of to experience this kind of classical levity is to turn on the TV to a football game, turn down the sound, and put on a Mozart string quartet. Do this and you'll begin to get what it is I'm referring to.

In a live concert improvisation, humor is very much linked to the drama and the kind of theatrical quality of the unstated boundaries or rules that often times restrict movement or acceptable methods of playing the instrument. For example: you're not supposed to stand up while you're playing; shouldn't play beneath the bridge or beat on the instrument; shouldn't express joy vocally or shouldn't laugh while playing, or even let your eyes glimmer while you are playing. These are some of the theatrical elements which seem to arise spontaneously when you really are enjoying what you are doing, musically. And they are all traditionally taboo. So, more than humor I guess, there is often, for me, a sense of light-heartedness, which emerges most often through improvising. And here, I'll reiterate again what a joy it is for me to make music! I am feeling most profoundly alive when I am doing this.

CROWE: I can't resist asking the question, "who are your heroes?" And how have these heroes influenced you and your music?

FRIESEN: Certainly one of the first as well as one of the greatest influences for me were my mother and father. Both were musicians—singers. My father was very dedicated to sacred music. My mother very dedicated to serving her family. Great "servants" and great models, both.

Pablo Casals was another hero. The great Catalonian cellist who brought the cello out of the closet, so to speak. Actually liberated the technique of the cello and made it an instrument that could be a more facile voice as a solo instrument. Because of his political views and having been exiled from Spain during the time of Franco, his focus turned to more human values. Much of his music is centered around the theme of peace. He closely associated the voice of the cello with the voice of a deeply human call to justice. And that stand, that focus and framework, has had a profound influence on me.

CROWE: Any heroes not directly associated with the music world?
FRIESEN: The contemporary American poet, novelist, essayist Wendell Berry has influenced my worldview. Primarily in terms of his sense of connection to place. His ability to see, in nature, the metaphors for religion and poetry. His human values, too, have affected me greatly.

And also Father Thomas Berry [no relation], whose book *The Dream of the Earth* [Sierra Club Books, 1989] mirrors and echoes some of my deeply felt instincts whereas the divinity of creation is concerned. His scale of universal divine essence is something I can very consciously and closely relate to. Also, his profound warning—his call to consciousness—for the saving of the planet from the inevitable cause-and-effect scenario of man's desecration of the natural world.

CROWE: Regarding the idea of humor in conjunction with the list of those who have influenced you in various ways, is there anyone in particular that you would like to name that has influenced you in terms of their waggishness alone?
FRIESEN: Some of the most spiritual people that I have known have been real party people. People who are able to laugh freely and eas-

ily. In fact, for me this has been the mark of people who are close to my idea of those who I would consider "heroes."

William Irwin Thompson, who is another very fun-loving person, comes to mind as someone I admire and have learned a great deal from. Wes Jackson [author of *The Roots of Agriculture*], who is a total crack-up, is someone who I have a great deal of respect for. Paul Winter has an amazing sense of humor. And it's probably the result of his sense of humor that has allowed us to manage to get through the last couple of decades together!

CROWE: Finally, let me ask what is your dream for the future of music and its audience?

FRIESEN: In terms of my vision for a musical future—my dream is of a participatory music. Huge liturgies of music which have people chanting as if they are a mountain range paying homage to the cosmos. A music which leaves everyone at the end standing around with tears rolling down their cheeks and dancing hand –in hand. I'd like audiences to be experiencing music as if they were witnessing the birth of a child. Granted, these are tall orders for a humble music maker such as myself, but you asked for a dream, and this is what I would like to see.

After many years it has become tiresome making a five-minute piece followed by applause from an audience who is sitting down. What I envision is a *participatory music* that involves people emotionally in some way and leaves them, as a result, vitally and forever changed.

CHARLES LLOYD

Sound Brahman

When I was living in San Francisco during the 1970s, I kept hearing the name of Charles Lloyd, as if he were northern California's best-kept secret. There was a kind of mystical association with the stories I heard surrounding the music and life of this man. The picture that I had conjured in my mind from hearing these stories was of a "wandering monk-musician." Myth had it that with a backpack full of ancient and esoteric wind instruments, he would sometimes just appear at events or gatherings to wow the crowd into reverie and trance. There didn't seem to be enough superlatives to describe Charles Lloyd coming from those who told their stories of personal encounters with this "shaman flutist." I seemed to always arrive where he had just been in those days, a day too late, never having the chance to hear him play.

It wasn't until some years later that I actually heard his music. I was recuperating from a near-fatal automobile accident, and a friend had sent me a tape to listen to while convalescing. "Music to heal by," she had written in the accompanying note. The tape was *Pathless Path* by Charles Lloyd. To make a long story short, I loved the calming, meditational essence of the recording, and in my mind at least, I consider my time spent listening to *Pathless Path* as an important part of my recovery process. At that time, Lloyd's most ethereal recording became one of my favorite collections of recorded music. And I would have to say it is still one of my favorites today.

So, in the summer of 1997 when I had the chance to finally attend a Charles Lloyd concert, I was more than ready to drive three hundred miles to hear him play. A live outdoor concert held in the Cistern at the College of Charleston was the perfect setting for a Charles Lloyd event: an open courtyard surrounded by nineteenth-century architecture, under the moss-laden branches of the old Spanish oaks, on a perfectly quiet moon-fed night. Lloyd's music on that evening, as performed by his quartet (comprising Bobo Stenson, Anders Jormin, and Billy Hart), from the very outset with his concert-opener "The Blessing," was reverential if not transfixing. By the end of "The Blessing" I knew I was in for a treat.

During the afternoon prior to the Charleston performance, I had contacted the concert promoters and had been able to set up an interview for the following morning just prior to the departure of Lloyd and his band for concert dates in Germany and Eastern Europe. There in his hotel suite in Charleston, amidst packing for a monthlong concert and recording tour of Europe, we had a chance to talk.

In the midst of incredible commotion, I was immediately amazed at the calm and composure of this man, and the quiet clarity with which he was able to focus on and answer my questions as he, at the same time, directed the organizational traffic of preparations being carried out by his wife, Dorothy Darr, for a midday plane flight. Despite the phone calls and the constant interruptions, he got right to the point, almost as if he knew, somehow, in advance, what it was I was going to ask. "This man, like his music, is tuned in," I remember thinking to myself as we began our conversation that morning. And a week later, while transcribing the tape of that conversation, this notion was strongly reinforced, as what went down onto paper seemed to substantiate the stories and superlatives I'd heard during my years living in northern California almost two decades before.

As the result of hearing his music firsthand, speaking with him, and conversation and letters I've since had with both him and his wife Dorothy, I'd have to say that among the many inherently creative men and women I have had the good fortune to meet over the course of my life, Charles Lloyd certainly ranks as one of the most memorable.

Charles Lloyd was born March 15, 1938, in Memphis, Tennessee, a rich ethnic mix of African, Cherokee, Mongolian, and Irish, into a family with great self-dignity that was never undermined by the racism of the time. He received his first saxophone at age nine and became hooked on jazz, listening to the late-night radio broadcasts of the 1940s to the giants of jazz who were to influence him so greatly: Charlie Parker, Coleman Hawkins, Lester Young, Billie Holiday, and Duke Ellington. He learned music from Memphis jazz notables like pianist Phineas Newborn, saxophonist George Coleman, and trumpet great Booker Little, who was Lloyd's closest childhood friend. As a teenager he worked as a sideman for bluesmen Johnny Ace, Bobby "Blue" Bland, Howlin' Wolf, and B.B. King when they played in Memphis.

Classical music also made an impression on the young Lloyd, so in 1956 he left Memphis and headed west to study music at the University of Southern California with the late Bartok expert Halsey Steven, receiving his masters degree in music in 1960. He received an equally important education at night on the ripe Los Angeles jazz club circuit of the late fifties, jamming with West Coast jazz outcasts like Ornette Coleman, Scott LaFaro, Don Cherry, Charlie Haden, and Eric Dolphy.

Lloyd immediately jumped into the New York scene of the early sixties, playing at the Five Spot, Birdland, Half Note, Jazz Gallery, and Village Vanguard. He lived in Greenwich Village and soon befriended many of the jazz masters he so admired: Coltrane, Monk, Mingus, Coleman Hawkins, and Miles, to name a few.

In 1964 Lloyd became a member of the Cannonball Adderley Sextet and also, in the same year, signed with CBS Records. In 1965 he was voted *Down Beat* magazine's "New Star." At the end of 1965 Lloyd left Cannonball Adderley and formed his own permanent quartet. After several shifts in personnel, he settled on a permanent lineup that introduced the jazz world to the brilliant talents of Keith Jarrett on piano, Jack DeJohnette on drums, and Cecil McBee on bass. The first release was a studio record, *Dream Weaver*, followed by *Forest Flower: Live in Monterey*, recorded at the Monterey Jazz

Festival in September 1966. *Forest Flower* quickly went gold and was heralded as the first jazz record to sell a million copies. The record received unprecedented airplay on the new free-form FM rock radio stations of the late 1960s that became the music beacons for a whole generation of young Americans experimenting with new lifestyles and dynamic change in society. The quartet was the first jazz group to appear at the famed Fillmore Auditorium in San Francisco and other rock palaces, sharing bills with Jimi Hendrix, Janis Joplin, Cream, the Grateful Dead, and Jefferson Airplane.

In 1967 Charles Lloyd was voted Jazz Artist of the Year by *Down Beat* magazine. The quartet's stature grew to the point where they were invited to tour throughout the world—the Far East, the Soviet Union, and the Eastern Bloc nations of Europe—often marking the first time these audiences had heard an American jazz group live in performance.

In 1969, after reaching the pinnacle of success in the music world, the Charles Lloyd Quartet disbanded. Lloyd, feeling exhausted from a decade on the road and the craziness of the late sixties, the pressures of fame and the music business, and the recent death of his mother, decided he was ready to pursue a quieter personal path. His longtime interest in Eastern traditions of religion slowly came to the forefront of his life and eventually became the main focus of his energies. During the 1970s he became reclusive, making only occasional recordings that were more in tune with his spiritual journey (*Pathless Path*). He eventually withdrew in 1973 to Big Sur and a secluded section of the central California coast where the Santa Lucia Mountains dive precipitously down into the Pacific Ocean and where such artists as Robinson Jeffers, Langston Hughes, Lawrence Ferlinghetti, Henry Miller, Jack Kerouac, Jean Varda, and Jaime de Angula had found personal and artistic refuge.

In 1981 a remarkable seventeen-year-old jazz pianist from France, Michel Petrucciani, arrived at Lloyd's Big Sur retreat with a mutual friend. Lloyd was so taken by Petrucciani's unique talent and being, that he was inspired to end his ten-year sabbatical from the concert stage and return to active music making. The result was records such as *Montreux* and *A Night in Copenhagen*, both recorded during the eighties.

The Charles Lloyd Quartet that included Bobo Stenson, Anders Jormin, and Billy Hart made its first American tour in June 1993, beginning a new life for the look and sound of Lloyd's music. Having signed with ECM Records in 1990, and after his first recording *Fish Out of Water* with the new label, the head of ECM, Manfred Eicher, made the public statement concerning Lloyd's music: "I really believe this is the refined essence of what music should be." Music publications such as *Down Beat* and *Jassthetik*, from Germany, added "a music of quiet joy, a jazz seventh heaven," and "one of the first great jazz recordings of the nineties."

In 1994 Lloyd and what he referred to at the time as his "permanent" band released *The Call*, an album that reaches even farther into the essence and the "still point" of sound that has been so elusive to Lloyd over his lifetime yet, it would seem, so close at hand. Since then, Charles Lloyd has produced a number of new CDs, has played major jazz festivals and venues across the U.S. and Canada, and has toured the world. Most recently, he was invited to play at the Nobel Peace Prize ceremonies in Oslo, Norway, which honored Al Gore and his colleagues for their work in educating the world on the issue of global warming.

There's this story of a man who had lost his most valuable possession. He was out in the yard where he lived, searching for this lost object when a friend comes by and asks him, "What are you doing?" The man who is searching replies, "I've lost a very valuable jewel, and I'm looking for it." The friend then asks, "Where did you lose it?" The man who had lost the jewel again responds, "I lost it in the house." The friend says, "Well, why are you looking out here in the yard under the lamppost?" To which the searching man replies, "Well, this is where the light is."

—*story told by Charles Lloyd*

THOMAS RAIN CROWE: Last night, when you took the stage for the concert at the Cistern at College of Charleston, the big clock on the old building behind the stage just stopped. I was, for whatever reason, watching it, and was aware that it had stopped. Given the nature of your performance, the spiritual and uplifting quality of the pieces you performed, I felt that somehow there had to have been a connection between your music and the fact that the clock had stopped. The energy of the evening was, indeed, as if time was standing still. Perhaps emphasizing the idea that what you are doing, or at least trying to do, is timeless.

CHARLES LLOYD: No, I wasn't aware that the clock stopped when we took the stage last night. But that's a good place to start. For time doesn't really exist anyway. At least on a certain level of life. Perhaps in a relative sort of way, there is time—but when the music is happening it sort of removes the time. The Buddha, in terms of right-mindfulness, speaks about the qualities of Nowness. There is only the Now, he says. And so, if the clock stopped as you say, then that was quite a benediction.

CROWE: Your album *Pathless Path* has always been something of a signature piece for me—even though it has been largely ignored by the so-called serious music critics. In terms of this musical and spiritual path of yours, where do you see it as beginning?

LLOYD: Ever since the beginning, since I was born into this world, there have been things that I've been unable to understand. Like how I got dropped off into Memphis. Like they say: "Be careful how you choose your parents." [Laughs.] But when I look back in terms of my early contact with prophets, it's very beautiful. There was this source thing. There was this real elixir and essence of musicality.

There was this young genius, Phineas Newborn, who was like a young Art Tatum, and very inspirational during my early years. Newborn and music became like my religion. I saw this in the great music makers. I saw them as sages and saints. I saw them as transforming reality, as making a better world as a result of what they did musically.

I've known since the time I was three that I was to be a music maker. I was in a hot spot of something special going on with this indigenous art form of so-called "jazz." And, since the beginning, I've always been moved by that.

Again, when the music's happening, there's no sense of time. I remember I used to stand outside the clubs and listen to these musicians play, and I would literally just shake, you know, because I'd be so moved, profoundly moved. At the time I was too young on a normal level to know what those feelings of being transported were all about. But nevertheless, it happened. From the outset, from the age of being a very young child, I was always trying to understand truth, love. Asking questions about who I am, and why I was here. Trying to get to the essence of matter in things. I always felt a deep religiosity in the sense of being a seeker. I always wanted to know the ineffable, the Soul of All Souls. And it seems that in this lifetime I've always carried with me that burning quest. And so music for me was a door, an opening to a place of higher consciousness. And I've just always pursued the muse in that. In the music. You see, I always had, from a very young age, certain guides helping me along. There was this Phineas Newborn, that I mentioned. I remember playing in an amateur show when I was about ten. My performance generated tumultuous applause, and won me first prize. But when I came off the stage, this guy who was about six or seven years older than me, and whose presence you could literally see, took me by the shoulders, looked at me and said, "You need lessons, bad!" In terms of his being a guide, his statement sort of tempered me (with all the adulation of the moment) and saved me from my own potential sense of self-importance. He saved me from the early glare of the spotlights, from the mistaken identity of ego. This gesture from Newborn took me quickly and directly to quality. And I was up for it. You know it's said in the text: "whatever you are looking for is looking for you also."

So Newborn took me to this saxophone player who had a very beautiful sound. And in that sound—getting back to the thing you were addressing about time—time *did* stop for me. Do you know the expression "sound Brahman?" Brahman is a name for God, for an unmanifested, impersonal and absolute existence of Godhead. And then there's "the sound." Music makers have this ability, if they're really deep seekers, to hear the sound. Do you know the name Glenn Gould? He had a beautiful sound. Charlie Parker had a beautiful sound. Lady Day, Billie Holiday, had a beautiful sound. Lester Young, Coleman Hawkins, John Coltrane, Ben Webster . . . so many people have such beautiful sounds.

I grew up with a contemporary, Booker Little, who died too young at the age of twenty-three. He had a very pure beautiful sound. I always had this sound thing. And in the sound so much is revealed to you. And the deeper you get into it, the more it opens itself to you. Then it begins to speak to you about character. As I say, I've always been a dreamer. Always had a sense of mission. As a young man I was already trying to change the world with music. To make it a better and more beautiful place. A place of harmony where we could realize our high ideals. Where we could rise up to our full potential without false impediments. A place where culture, education and pathways are important.

I had this quartet with Keith Jarrett, Jack DeJohnette, and Cecil McBee. We were traveling around the world, and we had great success, and yet—and this was at the end of the sixties—in 1969 my mom died. I was thirty, and I had been reading *The Light of Asia*, which is the story of the life of Buddha, which was timely in that this was the first time that I had really faced my mortality. I had faced it when Booker died. He died at the age of twenty-three, and we were about the same age. And this was shocking, because when you're very young you don't think about your death. At least in those days, in my generation you didn't so much. Today, though it's different. These are different times. Kids today are surrounded with all types of violence and prefabricated death, if not the real thing. So I'm worried about our culture and what the modern experience is doing to, or not doing for, our young people. If you don't water the roots of the tree it's not going to grow properly. You see, my interest has always been in the largest macro notion that we are our brother's keeper. And I can't seem to shake these kinds of ideals that I've always had.

CROWE: What part does education, do you think, play in your musical ideals and worldview?

LLOYD: The thing about education that is most interesting to me is the business of imparting inspiration through a loving connection. From this approach, both the children and the teacher can gain so much from each other. During my first three years of school, I went to a Catholic school. The nuns used to beat me on the hands and keep me after school. Because of all this, I couldn't find my balance. I couldn't communicate. Fortunately the next year I went to a public school. In the fourth grade I had this teacher named Mrs. Handy, who was a very warm, soulful, and loving teacher. In her class that year a light came on inside me, and I became a little "genius" at mathematics. . . . you know, I knew all the answers and stuff. This was always in me, but it took something special to bring it out. So I'm concerned about the nurturing process that does or doesn't go on in our lives. We're all kind of orphans here. This isn't really our home. We're just passing through. You know . . . don't feel you need to build houses on this bridge.

All this is a long way 'round to getting back to the fact that I'm always working with "the sound." As I was saying earlier, there are many different people in many different fields who have had this beautiful sound. Horowitz had it. Heifetz had it. Casals had it. In the morning in Big Sur, I love to listen to Pablo Casals play the Bach cello suites.

CROWE: Are you trying to suggest that your quest for "the sound" is something of a Grail quest? An Einsteinian search for a musical "unified field"?

LLOYD: I wanted to change the world with music. But knowledge shatters on the hard rock of ignorance here in the relative world. So you have to pace yourself in how you proceed through this asylum, this gymnasium of life. So after my mom died, and as I was in the midst of the adulation being thrown down on my quartet, I realized that I wanted to change my character. Looking into the mirror of my soul I asked if maybe I shouldn't be beginning that transformation at home, and to really get deep with working on my character. So it was clear to me then that I needed to be conscious of those things, those people who come through our lives and touch us, who move us. I respond to this, and am moved by those examples. For me personally, they mostly occur with saints and sages, with avatars, and of course, with music makers. So the music was the opening and the catalyst to my diving deeper within.

CROWE: I'm very interested in this "diving within" aspect of your character and your life. I'm referring to the period after all this adulation you're talking about with the quartet, when you, quite literally, turned your back on that success and more or less disappeared into the coastal landscape of California. This was the early 1970s. I was living in San Francisco during the seventies, publishing a Beat poetry magazine called *Beatitude*, which was started by Bob Kaufman in the fifties, organizing large poetry events, but mainly just being a young poet in his twenties. Every once in a while, through the grapevine, stories of this wandering, monkish jazz flute player would make their way into town, and the legend of Charles Lloyd began to take hold for many of us younger "Baby Beats" as we were being called. Your reputation in our artistic circles quickly became mythic, and I was fascinated then as I am now to know more about that phase of your life.

LLOYD: I had actually "found my medicine" so to speak earlier. In my studying and contacts with the East. The thing that enthralled me about the East was that it taught me about Being and Becoming. Living in a society with all these negatives coming at you all the time, it was an interesting way for me to avoid not being run over by a Mack truck, so to speak. Something to work on, that also works on me. I'm always looking to be active. For something to work on. Especially if The Dance isn't happening on a level of The Divine.

But let me say something about this notion of my being a legend or my life being in some way mythic. I'm just a messenger. I'm just a vehicle. I don't want to be home in terms of that adulation. Don't get we wrong. I love the communion and the community of being a music maker. Like last night during our Spoleto concert—at a certain point I felt that everyone there was at home, was at home with a certain feeling. Even though everyone there was coming from different places geographically and in terms of consciousness, I could tell when we all had a commonality of "the touch" and "the tone." What I'm trying to tell you is that I have to be careful. There's a story of this guy who had this beautiful garden . . . he was always cultivating his flowers and plants with reverence for their beauty and for the Creator that had made them. One day, out of nowhere, an elephant found its way into the garden and trampled all the flowers. Where he had been one and at peace in the garden all these years, with this violation of his garden by the elephant, his anger returned. After years of being an enlightened sage-of-the-garden, in a single moment his mantle of discipline was shattered. When the gardener saw what the elephant had done, he took a machete and killed the elephant. A few days later the Creator came to this man's garden in the form of a human. "Is this your garden?" the Creator asked the gardener. "Yes," replied the gardener. "Did you grow all these flowers?" the Creator asked again. "Oh, yes, I grew everything in this garden," the man replied, taking great pride and credit for everything he had restored to the garden. "And did you kill this elephant?" the Creator finally asked. But the gardener did not want to take credit for what he had done to the elephant, even though he recognized in that moment that he, indeed, was not responsible for the creation of the flowers and the beauty of the garden.

With this story in mind, I have to always be mindful and aware that I am not becoming seduced by the strokes or something. I'm trying to stay simple and as humble as possible, you see, because the music that comes through—all I can do is hold on, because it's such a welcome touch of the miraculous that I feel like I have to break out in song. Do you know Tagore? It's like some of the stuff he writes about—lines come to mind like: "O my heart, I call thee friend who art my Lord." Like Tagore, I feel that I am a servant. I serve the music. You know, then there is that certain place you arrive at by being a willing servant to the music, that you get so high from it that you actually find yourself there face to face with the Creator saying, "Hi friend"—talking to the Lord.

CROWE: Your story and the story of your relationship with the music reminds me of another conversation I had a couple years ago with a blind painter named Lyn Ott. De Kooning said of him, back in the fifties, at the height of the Abstract Expressionist explosion: "He's the only one of us who can paint!" Much like yourself, in the face of imminent stardom, he turned his back on the whole New York art scene, and ran off to India—"in search of the face of God"—to use his own metaphor. And then spent the remaining fifteen years of his sighted life painting what he believed was the face of God. For fifteen years, trying to reach the essence of his creative medium and at the same time, of the physical and non-physical universe. Does this story have any resonance for you in terms of what you are striving to achieve with your music?

LLOYD: Yes, same thing. You see, everyone who dives deep into this thing we call spirituality finds the same thing. The first thing you realize is that you can't take authorship for what you create. And the whole thing of "name and fame," it's like a hog plum. Do you know this expression? A hog plum is a plum with all pit and skin. There's no juicy fruit inside. On the other hand, there are those who really get off on name and fame. But don't get me wrong, there's something really wonderful about being appreciated, and about the applause . . . but there's more than that. Like when that special something happens that blesses the whole. . . . It's true that I went away for a long time, and during that time, I'll admit, I did miss some of that adulation, but at the same time, I thought during this period of "silence," that maybe I could get together with myself, get myself together, you see, in maybe six months, or maybe a year. So I went to Big Sur to hang out with myself and the beauty of nature, and a couple of decades went by. And during all that time I only got a glimpse of what I started out looking for. But that glimpse has been so powerful that I can't go back. I've been bit by the cobra, now, and that experience has changed, forever, the way I see things. At least I hope there's no turning back, because, you see, we're all hypnotized here. We think we build an angel and she turns out to be just some guy named Harold. . . . [Laughs.] It's nonsense. And when you get to the point where you *know* that it's nonsense, and you've opened up into that Nowness, and are being mindful, observant. . . . There's this story about Buddha, where one of his disciples came to him one day flustered and frustrated and says: "Master, I can't do all these things you say I must do. There are too many precepts. You ask me to do all these precepts, and I can't do all these things!" The Buddha looked at the disciple and said, "You say that you can't do all these precepts, well, can you do one?" The disciple looks at Buddha and says, "Well, yes, maybe I can do one. What is it?" The Buddha looks at the disciple and says "Right-mindfulness," the point being here, that if you can do right mindfulness, you don't have to worry about the others.

Beyond this, I really don't know what to say, except that I really don't know much. Let me put that differently. I don't know anything. That's just getting more and more clear to me. As a young man, I thought I knew a lot of stuff; thought I knew it all. [Laughs.] Boy, if that wasn't the height of stupidity! Life is as interesting as it is cruel.

CROWE: In 1990 you released a recording titled *Fish Out of Water*. After the years spent outside of the music scene, then having re-turned, is this title an apt metaphor for how you saw yourself upon return, or might it be telltale in some way for where you find your-self now?

LLOYD: I'm not exactly sure how I came up with that title. That re-cord was a cathartic experience for me. It was at the time that my manager had gotten me a deal to record with ECM in Germany, thinking that they would be receptive to my music and would al-low me to work in the way I do, that really runs at right angles to the whole recording industry. You know, the business of music. You see, I'm really a musician more by nature than by profession. I break out into song, then I disappear into the woods for twenty years. The big record execs can't handle that kind of temperament. "How is he going to build a career?" they would be yelling. I'm not interested in that path. If you go with your higher self and with your truth, whatever that may be, and you're sincere, the Mother will take care of you. I believe this, and so I'm not concerned, like the execs, about how am I going to survive, and I'm not making my musical decisions based on this kind of focus. I mean, why shouldn't God, or the Mother, provide? Provide for our deepest and sincerest needs. We're not talking about shopkeeping, about asking God for things. You have to have an infinite communion with whatever that spiritual force is you're addressing, for this approach to work.

It's a lot like getting in touch with the sound. Get deep off into that . . . I mean, it makes complete sense. Like so many people, I'm not into renouncing the "real" for glass beads. People say things to me like, "Oh, those twenty years must have been so hard." It wasn't hard at all! So, having notions like these keeps moving me upward, in a sense. And yes, it does get rocky and craggy at times. And you're always slipping on banana peels on that razor's edge, so it can be a bit tricky. But I've found that you just have to keep what your practice is. It's like one of those wise guys like Yogi Berra said: "If you don't know where you're going, you might end up some-where else." [Laughs.]

CROWE: So there's got to be some discipline in that path somewhere. It's not just all spontaneity, free-flight, and bliss?

LLOYD: Absolutely! Discipline for me, man, is one of the keys to freedom. The ability to run has in it the inherent ability to walk, if you see what I mean. If there's not this, then you can't get the best transmission of what the message is. If everyone is not joyously there, you know, it's not happening. I like that high level of creativity. That universal that can articulate the personal truth. That's what this art form does for me; it articulates truth, which is a place one can find oneself.

CROWE: There are so many familiar points of connection for me with regards to your work, your life, your vision and your practice. Places, geography, people. . . . For instance, I lived for a year in Memphis when I was six years old. I dropped out of the "scene" in San Francisco (where I, too, spent some time down in Big Sur at Ferlinghetti's cabin) and went back to the North Carolina woods and disappeared, after realizing that I couldn't change the consciousness of America by exposing large audiences to visionary poetry. And then there is the story of a major automobile wreck I was involved in that left me essentially immobile for a couple years—years that I got through, in large part, from listening to your recording, *Pathless Path*, which came to me completely serendipitously.
LLOYD: Did you know Bob Kaufman when you were in San Francisco?

CROWE: Yes, very well. I was upstairs in Malvina's cafe when he broke his vow of silence, which had lasted some thirteen years. He jumped up on a table and began reciting Eliot, Olson, and Keats all intertwined. This remarkable recitation went on for several minutes. . . . I've never heard anything so astonishing before or since. Then, of course, he began giving readings again, to which hundreds, even thousands of people would come to hear this "Black Rimbaud," as the French refer to him. I spent some kind of time with him almost daily for some four and a half years. I'd have to consider him one of my major influences, if not teachers.

LLOYD: Just before we left on this trip a few days ago, we were look-ing at a beautiful photograph of Bob and me that was taken of us together. I've been really blessed in this lifetime. I've known a lot of people who are really working with "It." And you know, when you say something to me about something like your story of *Pathless Path*, in a way it reverberates for me as a warm feeling, because I'm like a troubadour—I pass through here, and I sing my song, and I'm gone. I don't have any instant feedback, other than the nowness of the moment, about the effect of my work. My dreams are big-ger than my memories, you know, and I'm still just trying to make music, to be a music maker.

CROWE: Just as I look to artists like Bob Kaufman as creative and spiritual teachers, whom would you sight as your teachers?

LLOYD: My guru was a musician. He played the vina and the sarod. But this whole stream of deity and example that I follow . . . I've always found that they were involved in the arts. I don't mean to seem sectarian here, or to talk about a narrow path. I'm a universal-ist. If you've ever noticed in terms of rituals, you can find something that's done in Tibet that is also practiced on this continent by the Navajo, for example. The same holds true from India to Africa, those certain similarities in the way unassociated peoples honor the Creator. And there are many solar systems. Things aren't such a mystery, really. Yet, at the same time, and God bless paradox, they are mysterious depending on what level you're dealing with things. But I'm just trying to focus on being simple. I don't want to get caught up in being pedantic and talking about things that aren't just direct essence. The bottom line for me is that I'm simply trying to get to the distillation of essence.

CROWE: Well, you must be doing something right, as the head of your recording company, ECM, has compared your recent work to paintings by Giacometti, and has said that he believes that "this is the refined essence of what music should be." Then you, yourself, were quoted somewhere, I believe, as saying: "Here I am at this advanced stage of my life and I'm still trying to get to the essence of the tone, to the place where that quality of suchness or purity can came through. I'm still trying to be a musician. In music, I've never gotten good enough to quit." Do you recognize any of that, or is my memory, as you say, being overridden by my dreams?

LLOYD: In *Pathless Path*, that you say you liked, I was trying to impart something to the listener. There too, as in my other recordings, I was trying to get to the source of the essence of things musically.

CROWE: The music critics pretty much ignored *Pathless Path*, and by ignoring it were, as far as I could discern, passing it off as being unimportant in the context of your whole body of work. I've very curious what your relationship is with that recording, and the music you were making there.

LLOYD: It's all part of that quest for essence. That's just the music that I was making then. I made that recording and then they came along and started this thing they called "New Age." Fortunately, I did all this stuff and was gone before they put all those labels on my work.

This all reminds me of once upon a time when I was playing opposite Thelonius Monk at the Village Gate in New York, when I was just this precocious kid in my twenties and had had some modicum of success—and I had it written into my contract that I had to have fresh-squeezed orange juice to drink backstage, you know, with oranges no more than six hours off the tree, and all kinds of little things like that. And there was this Rothschild woman, this baroness, whose name was, I believe, Nica—one of the rich Rothschilds. Actually, now that I think of it, Charlie Parker died at her suite over at the Stanhope Hotel. Anyway, she was a patron of Monk's. And she'd drive him around in her Bentley and take him to gigs and stuff like that.

And so one night—getting back to this orange juice thing—I tasted my orange juice backstage one night, and it didn't taste fresh. It seemed spoiled to me. And Monk, who was kinda funny in his behavior—you know, he didn't talk in sentences like everyone else, and he'd just be dancin' off the walls with his deities and stuff, and you know, he'd just be in his world, you know, but he would drink my orange juice. So that night I told Nica, I said, "When Monk comes in, tell him not to drink my orange juice, 'cause it's spoiled." So eventually Monk showed up, and when he came in, Nica immediately started in with her high-pitched aristocratic English accent: [Lloyd imitates her voice, falsetto] "Oh, Thelonius. Oh, Thelonius. Charles says not to drink the orange juice; it's tainted." Monk didn't pay her any mind, he just kept circling the room, dancin' with his deities. And so finally, he made his way over to the pitcher of orange juice, and he picked it up, and he kind of eased over by me and he looked at me and downed the whole pitcher of juice. Then he looked at me again and said, "Tainted, huh?" then kind of danced off. . . . It was kind of like Milarepa. You hip to Milarepa?

CROWE: I've heard the name is all.

LLOYD: You hear of *The Hundred Thousand Songs of Milarepa?* This whole scene was like the great Tibetan saint, Milarepa. Monk had taken this poison and turned it into *soma*, and then laughed. A holy man can do that, and those examples for me were very powerful. Through those examples, I realized that I also had to get something together that fire couldn't burn and that water couldn't wet and wind wouldn't blow. . . . So, I'm still workin' on it.

CROWE: I just want to say here, that the first piece you guys did last night at the Cistern was mesmerizing. Rarely am I moved so deeply and so immediately by anything. Can you tell me what the title of that piece is?

LLOYD: It's called "The Blessing," and, truthfully, I rarely play that piece. It's on *The Call*. I think you'd really like my latest recording. I think you'd really respond to it, especially if you like a *Pathless Path* and "The Blessing." As I was saying to you earlier, all these are steps. Even the mistakes I've made are steps. You know what I mean? I've learned something from all of it, and Lord knows I've made detours.

It's all humbling. The key is to be aware enough . . . to realize that you need to watch out for the paint. And not to get into the space where you got to think that it was your hands that got in it, rather to realize that you were being used for this to come through. So if some guy wants to change the world, fine. . . . If he wants to take that on his shoulder, fine. We'll send some of that through him, too.

CROWE: Since we're on this line, or level, of conversation, there's something that I'd like to run by you. One of the things that has caught my attention over the years is a concept/idea that I call "radiogenesis." It has to do with transmission and translation in terms of the creative process. More specifically, it has to do with the material that seems more to come *through* you than come *from* you. Am I reading too much into what you're saying here, to assume that the "coming through" is more your process than the "coming from"?

LLOYD: I'm not sure if I understand maybe exactly where you're coming from with this, but it triggers something in me. We were talking about discipline earlier. If you look at life in general, most people are more or less blowin' in the wind—drifting, and reacting. I'm saying that it's the quality of what you can let go of, how empty you can be, how aware you can be, what you are inviting to come through consciously, that counts. I don't want to give the impression that the way I operate is that—whatever it is that comes through me, whatever garbage, is okay. You understand what I'm saying? It's not garbage in, garbage out with me, but at the same time, I'm open to whatever's out there, or inside of me that speaks to my highest ideals for myself and the planet, but to harness all that with discipline. For me, it's about quality—always quality.

CROWE: Let me take this idea of "radiogenesis" a little further. I believe that if there was some sort of universal Rosetta stone where you could translate, directly, image and metaphors and rhythmic language into musical notation, or if you could directly translate certain choreographic body movement, or the use of light and color on canvas into symbolic language, and if you took some of the great masters in all the art forms—the Mozarts, the Bachs, the Beethovens, the Raphaels, the Michelangelos, the DaVincis, the Nijinskys, the Duncans, the Blakes, the Rimbauds, the Dantes—that much of what all these guys are "saying" may be exactly the same. It just comes out in different forms, through a different process of transmission and transmutation. You see what I'm getting at here?

LLOYD: Yes, I think I understand where you're coming from with this, but I have to say that it's my feeling that music is much deeper than the other art forms—not to take anything away from those other ways of expression. You mentioned that listening to the quartet last night, it brought tears to your eyes when we were playing "The Blessing." I can't even remember the last time we played that piece in concert. Not this year, I'm certain. "The Blessing" is not the kind of piece that you can just start out playing, flat or unprepared. You have to really warm up to that piece, and be in the space where that higher level of transmission can come through. And I really don't know why I chose to play "The Blessing" last night and not any other time this year. Everything, I guess, has to be just right for those magic moments to occur. And, how that happens has more to do with intuition and spontaneous, in-the-moment decision making based on how and what I'm feeling, seeing around me. And last night I guess everything was in proper alignment for me to want to play the piece, and for the piece to come off the way you say it did.

CROWE: I want to say something here about your relation to the other members of the quartet and the way you all play together, the way you collaborate. I guess what struck me most strongly was the qualities of the silences in your work with the other guys in your group—Bob Stenson, Anders Jormin, and Billy Hart—the patience and the willingness to wait for the next notes and tones, and yet at the same time, doing this without any sense of there being "dead space." The level of sensitivity between the four of you approaches sensuality while implying an inherent sense of conversational harmony. Does it feel as good for you up there as it does for those of us in the audience?

LLOYD: That *is* the great joy for me, to show up somewhere and to allow this music thing to just happen. We played down in Atlanta just before we came up to Charleston for last night's concert. We played there for 25,000 standing! You talk about getting charged up! And wanting to believe your own press or something . . . those kinds of moments can really take you off the road if you're not careful. But I was really moved by that. As far as I could see out in front of me, people were on their feet showing their appreciation for what we had done. Something must have been moving out there for that kind of show of affection.

I believe that these kinds of things have an effect. Maybe it slowed some young person down just enough where they didn't go out and do something violent, adding to all the plight and pain we have today in our society.

It's a growing, living organic music, and this is the first group I've had where it's just total harmony of integration of what's said, of what's lived, and what's played. Don't get me wrong—all my groups have been made up of people who were always the best that they could be, but this group is somehow good for my character, for the more true my character can become, the easier it becomes for everyone in the group—to work on the tone, you know. And that seems to be what is happening with this group.

CROWE: Yes, the thing that stands out, for me, with the four of you onstage, which includes the sound, or the "tone" as you say, is a pervading sense of calm. Even with the quick stuff, there is an ever-present sense of calm.

LLOYD: Yes, you have to have that restful alertness.

CROW: I kept making comparisons to Hendrix all during your performance last evening. Others might say, "there is no sense of calm in Hendrix," but there is!

LLOYD: Of course!

CROWE: Now we're getting into the area of shamanism, of creative cause and effect. A little story: The blind blues harmonica player, Sonny Terry, one night several years ago up in South Bend, Indiana, through some conscious manipulation on both his part and mine, hit what I have to call a "transcendent" high note on his D harp and cured my brother, who is a visual artist, a painter, of a potentially career-threatening eye disease he had developed. I believe this. I believe these things are possible. Not everything is coincidence, and there's something poetically believable about a blind man healing the blind.

I'm also interested in the physics of this kind of healing, and so I'm interested, I guess, in how you see your relationship with this kind of work with the muse.

LLOYD: I'm here just to play music, to get out of the way and let the music come through. Obviously, as you point out, these things have some effect, and these things do happen. It's true that yesterday I was called here in Charleston by an Atlanta radio station who chased me over here telling me that they had had so many calls after the Atlanta concert—people wanting to talk to me about the music—that they (the radio station) wanted me to do an hour call-in interview show over the phone, long-distance. So I talked for an hour to the people of Atlanta who had, they said, been moved by our performance there.

You know, it seems strange for me now, thinking back to that little kid that I was with the big vision and not knowing how it would manifest, to be witness to how my work sometimes touches people. As I say, it's humbling. At the same time, because I have this gift, I have this responsibility of getting out of the way and of trying to remain untainted by that gift. You know, like the orange juice thing with Monk. Instead of becoming the sour juice, to transform that "tainted" juice, or ego, back to pure essence.

CROWE: I've asked everyone I've interviewed for this book, if they have a good, epiphanal story which pertains to their own life and their own musical development. So I'd like to ask you the same question: Is there a story of epiphany which comes to mind that you'd like to share?

LLOYD: I don't know if I know how to answer that, but at the same time, there are many incidents in my life that I guess you could say were life-changing on some level. The most recent, I suppose, was back in 1986 when I almost died. I was having surgery for an intestinal thing and I was diagnosed as only having eleven hours to live. The interesting, and possibly the epiphanal thing about that story is that I almost welcomed that news. I was prepared to go. I had made my peace. I liked that. I liked something about the fact that I had a warning: "Hey, you've got a few hours left here." It was a gift, really. Most people don't have that kind of warning. Their car is hit in a car accident and wham, they're out of the body.

When my guru, Swami Ritajananda, was dying . . . one day, when his disciples were in the hospital where they were keepin' him, and they were all hovering over him wondering when he would die . . . he got tired of all the commotion and sat up and said, "Look, I'll let you know when it's time; I'll let you know when it's time." Now you've got to understand that as a spiritual teacher, this man had been getting ready all his life to die. So to him, this was not a big deal; he'd been preparing for this moment all his life. So the doctors had him in the hospital trying to keep him alive, and all the while he had made up his mind that it was time for him to go. Well, he would leave the final exit, and they had him on all these machines and he was all tied up with IV tubes and all . . . and one day when all the disciples were hangin' around there in his room, he came back into his body from being out-of-body, and looked up at everyone and said: "Well, I'm trying to leave, but I can't because of all these things all over me!"

So, you see, it's about getting out of the way, again. In this case, it's getting all that technology out of the way and letting a holy man exercise his will and go on. A holy man can do that.

And in my case in 1986, I was in a similar situation where they had told me that I was about to die, and I had made peace with that and with my life and with the world. The experience of this was a kind of epiphany for me. Because, as you can see, I didn't die, yet had the gift of going through a dry run of the whole death thing. And that has changed the way I have seen and walked through life these past six or seven years. So we're trying to live a simple life like that, and not say a lot about it, you know.

Now you've got me thinking about these things . . . and I'm remembering. There were many things. When I was young and wild, I was driving my Ferrari in upstate New York, and it was one of these days that was cold and wet, and the road was a sheet of ice, and I hit a big patch of ice going quick in that Ferrari, and there were huge chasms on both sides of the road, and there was no way around the curves on that ice for me to avoid going down into those chasms, but somehow the Mother just brought me on into the city. . . . Many times. One time I was driving in a snow-storm in New Mexico or somewhere, in the early sixties. A big tractor trailer had jackknifed right in front of us—a big semi—and there was nowhere to go. The whole band was driving together in those days to gigs in a station wagon. When that trailer jackknifed in front of us and we were going right at it, we all looked at each other as if it was the last thing we'd ever do. We looked at each other all at the same time, and when we looked up we were on the other side of the trailer, stretched out vertically across the road. No one ever talked about it. No one wants to touch something like that. [Laughs.]

These kinds of things made me realize that I had some important work to do. You know, it wasn't my time. I wasn't finished here yet. Right before we went out on the road this time, I had a dream. It was an incredible dream. In fact it was more than a dream; it was something of a vision—that the music was coming through again, and I was to serve it. It was direct. I don't know. I'm no poet. I can't use words like Kaufman, but it was clear; I could see it as clear as I see you. Mother was right there with me and just let me know that this is my work and it's okay, and I have to do it and not bother about it, and it was just very moving—and the word "responsibility" came to me during this vision.

I'm getting to be an elder almost now, and so I have to take on that mantle, although I still feel young and precocious. But with all the close calls I've gone through just to be here for this chance at playing music, I've got to not squander my gifts, so to say.

CROWE: So, now that you're back, so to speak, how do you feel? Do you still feel like a fish out of water?

LLOYD: When I did the recording *Fish Out of Water*, it was representative of how I was feeling then. I hadn't made a record in several years—a live studio record. You know, whatever it is that I do, it's not "legal." I've always known that the truth's in the music—the deep truth. Like when I played in Russia in 1967. I was told that I was the first musician ever to be invited by the people to come to Russia. My trip and performance there was not sanctioned by the government—and this was in 1967—at the height of the Vietnam War—but by some music society. When we arrived there, they told us that we wouldn't be allowed to play because the Americans had escalated the war in Vietnam. And I said to them, "Why would I want to be involved in any way with that? That's not my mission. I'm a musician." And they asked me, finally, did I want to go on TV, to teach classes on jazz, and all kinds of other things, and I just said "No, I'm here to be with warm, breathing human beings who want to hear this music, and we're going to play this music for them." Well, finally after three days of these stalling tactics to keep us from playing, I asked the people in charge: "Are you practicing racism here?" And this question really blew them out, 'cause they didn't want to be tainted with that stigma. And their attitude changed instantly, and they were almost begging me to play at that point. It's so strange dealing with politicians. They can only relate to certain levels, a certain dynamic of reality.

About my coming back this time, and I've been gone a long time, the important thing is that you bring something back. I hope that what I do can inspire people.

CROWE: Well, one way to look at it is, that the very fact that you're out on the road and doing it is an indication that you're in the water again.

LLOYD: Yes, that part is true, most definitely! I am back. The hiatus is over. What happened was that in being gone for so long, I got really friendly with solitude. The adulation of the crowd is not that narcotic for me. Enlightenment, itself, is not really that flashy. It's really a quiet kind of thing—not the rush everyone thinks it's supposed to be. It's really deep, you know, every pore. . . . . It's not a localized kind of thing. It takes a lot of quiet thinking to know that and apprehend that. What little glimpses I've had of that have propelled me forward. I have been blessed to be with someone who cares for me greatly and we're on the path together. I don't know a lot. I just get up in the morning and try to tie my shoes like everyone else. The difference is, that I do it now with a kind of grace that I didn't have as a young man. Everything I did then was done with a sense of bravura. Not to negate that music, or my life then—it was all the same thing. But now, I have a little better sense of something about it.

So I hope that there are a lot of us that are "fish out of water," that are sensitive in that way. My whole theory is that there are a lot of people, a lot of souls on the planet who are much more sensitive than they're given credit for. There's all this hype about Madison Avenue and about all the politicians who are leading us around. I think that self-actualization is something that is in all of us. We just need a spark. As for me, I just play this music.

ABDULLAH IBRAHIM

Transcending the Blues

first came across Abdullah Ibrahim in Ken Franckling's article "Going Home," in *Down Beat* (October 1992). What stood out was the quote in the box: "Improvisation is meditation in motion." Those words made me want to hear this man's music. Looking through all the great titles like *Mantra Mode* (Enja, 1991), *Streams of Consciousness* (Bay, 1977), and *African Dawn* (Enja, 1982), I got hold of Ibrahim's solo album *Desert Flowers* (Enja, 1990), and on first hearing, I was brought into the world of his South African heritage and was under his spell.

It turns out that Ibrahim started life as Adolphus Brand in the colored district of Kensington, Cape Town, South Africa. There in the rich mix of traditional and urban music he heard as a child, he grew up playing piano, both native music and gospel, in the local A.M.E. church and singing spirituals and hymns in the church choir. He says the music of the Cape of South Africa is "so wide, it's difficult to describe." It included the music of the bushmen—the *khoisan* people—and the Cape Muslims who were originally brought there as slaves. And there was also the American and British pop music that the local musicians played with a Cape Town beat. In those days he hung out with the merchant seamen coming into port who brought jazz records from the United States, giving him exposure to Duke Ellington and other American artists from the pre-bop era. It was from buying those cheap dollar records from the merchant seamen that he got the nickname "Dollar Brand."

His first professional job in high school was as pianist in a traditional dance band. It was a regular jump band that played a mix of Western arrangements and traditional music for South African audiences who believed that music was made for dancing. In 1959, the young Dollar Brand made musical history in South Africa by co-founding the Jazz Epistles with trumpeter Hugh Masekela. The Jazz Epistles were the first South African jazz band to record all original material.

In 1962 at age twenty-eight, Dollar Brand left his beloved South Africa with his wife, singer Sathima Bea Benjamin, leaving the repression of apartheid behind and searching out opportunities for making music in Europe. Their first stop was Zurich, where chance would have it that Duke Ellington came through, heard his trio perform, and recorded them in 1963 in Paris for Reprise on *Duke Ellington Presents the Dollar Brand Trio*. By 1965, Brand and his wife had moved to New York. Ellington sponsored them at the Newport Jazz Festival, and later Brand substituted for Ellington on tour. In the late sixties he continued expanding his horizons by converting to Islam and taking the name Abdullah Ibrahim. He toured Europe as a soloist and in groups that included trumpeter Don Cherry, drummer Makaya Ntshoko, and bassist Johnny Gertze.

The seventies, eighties, and early nineties saw Ibrahim composing and performing his own music—simple yet sophisticated, tranquil yet transforming—in many parts of the world. He performed both as a soloist and in duos with Max Roach and Carlos Ward, as well as with his trio and with his septet Ekaya (meaning "home"). His base in those years was the Chelsea Hotel in New York. From there he has toured in the U.S., Europe, South America, and Asia. Upon his return to South Africa in 1976 and after the Soweto uprising that year (performing at his first political benefit for the African National Congress), Ibrahim and his wife chose voluntary exile from South Africa in protest against apartheid. During these years, along with his performing schedule, he made nearly two hundred recordings. It wasn't until 1992, when Mandela was released from prison and elected president of the Republic of South Africa, that Ibrahim returned to make music in his native land and to take an active part in the rebuilding of community there through his gift of music.

It was on a warm moonlit night in May 1998 that we caught Abdullah Ibrahim and his trio—bassist Marcus McLaurine and drummer George A. Johnson Jr.—playing in the jazz spotlight at the Cistern in Charleston, South Carolina, as a headliner for the Spoleto USA Festival. In one long, timeless set, their own serene style of acoustic fusion sang out through the live oaks and into the bay. Beginning with a township tune from Maraba, near Pretoria, Ibrahim threaded the melody through sophisticated harmonies in homage to Ellington and Coltrane, weaving in subtle African rhythms along the way. The magic of the music transported the crowd of eager jazz fans into a distant realm, transcending the blues of memory with the hope of promise.

The next morning, Ibrahim took some time out of his busy summer schedule—he would perform again that evening and return to South Africa later in the week—to talk to Nan Watkins and me. We found him in his hotel room surrounded by his homeopathic medicines—he was fighting a cold—and swaddled in Turkish towels. Abdullah Ibrahim was patiently and quietly answering the questions of a local radio reporter. Bidding the man good-bye, he rose to welcome us, and slowly he began to tell his stories of how his chosen path of music has led him to what he calls his "songs of praise."

NAN WATKINS: I was moved by your performance under the trees at the Cistern here in Charleston last night—your performance seemed one long and beautiful meditation. As a keyboard musician myself, I find the salient characteristic of your music to be its calm, its serenity. Can you describe the source, the wellspring of that serenity?

ABDULLAH IBRAHIM: Let me put it this way. I have been studying the so-called martial arts for close to thirty years. I started this as a kind of discipline. As a musician, you have to have discipline. So I started getting involved with karate. I have an excellent teacher in Japan. This study focuses on the transformation of an external system into an internal system. The principle of the internal system is strength—soft outside and strong within—as opposed to the external system which is about muscular power. If one plays only externally, I find that it's very, very stressful because in some ways you are playing with muscular energy. It is not necessary to use external forces. It's almost contradictory. That's the principle that I apply to playing. There is a greater effect by playing internally rather than externally.

WATKINS: Your music last night seemed to inscribe a musical circle. You have referred to music as spirit and have called music "an unseen art." That all seems to come together here, playing from the strength within.

Now, let me ask a more particular question about key color or tone color. Do you have any private theories about certain tones that you feel are more spiritual or in tune with the spirit than others? I heard a lot of flats, D-flats and A-flats, last night, or was this just my imagination?

IBRAHIM: We've been using the scale as by Pythagoras. Part of our studies takes us into this whole theory of right angle triangles. The square of the hypotenuse is equal to the sum of the squares of the other two sides. If you apply that principle, then you end up with semitones. If we extend this principle, we arrive at the triangle. A pyramid. A pyramid is exactly two right-angle triangles. Back to back. From the base of the triangle to the apex two-thirds of the way up is an energy field. In principle, this will give you the equivalent of what is called the Golden Mean or the Golden Section. Now, we work with this principle which is injected into the music. In a way, the formula is utilized.

When I speak to my friends in the building trade, we talk about harmonics. The basic ratio of harmonics is 3-5-7. You apply the same principle of the right triangle to building, and this is connected to sound the same as it applies to architecture. This applies to things that are seen and unseen. This is the research. The idea of movement as it relates to the martial arts. And sound. Although sound is not necessarily mathematics, it has a direct relationship with physics and is all relative in that sense. In fact, I am revising Einstein's Theory of Relativity: $E=mc^2$. It equates to the metaphysical theory: God is Light.

WATKINS: I'm curious here. Are you familiar with the writings of Hazrat Inayat Khan, the Sufi musician and teacher-philosopher?
IBRAHIM: Oh, we know him. We know the book *The Mysticism of Sound* and all the ten volumes he is known for. The idea is that if you think logically, you have to arrive at that point. The problem is that the information that we receive at the beginning of our lives, that information is not quite correct. We cannot come to a logical conclusion, because our basic information is warped. So we always arrive at the wrong point.

WATKINS: How do you think we should go about changing that basic information for the young? What can we do to help put them on the right track?
IBRAHIM: Right now, in South Africa, we are creating music academies. There will be one in Cape Town and one in Johannesburg, with the idea that music is the core. There we will investigate the links with music and the other subjects. We are working internationally with music people all over the world. It is this kind of information that we need to reintroduce. There is a relationship here with medicine. My great-grandfather was an herbal healer. Doctors in South Africa now will give you a choice between antibiotics and homeopathic cures. This sort of thing is accepted in South Africa. These things are happening side by side.

WATKINS: Is your work with these music academies going to take a lot of your time personally?
IBRAHIM: No, I was very smart. I have an army of helpers and assistants. They gave me a title of Creative Director. I said, "That's fine, as long as I don't have to attend meetings." [Laughs.] We've been blessed with such a fantastic response from people who want to work on this project. And I also think that people in the teach-

ing profession are beginning to look further afield. Our system is changing. There are tremendous problems, and the blessing is that it's now possible to change the system. Possible to change it right from the ground up. Change the structures. Reinvent them. Reset them. This is a great opportunity.

WATKINS: You were talking earlier about how, in the culture that you're from, the medicine tradition and the music tradition are linked in terms of apprenticeship and the whole process. In the past you have spoken about what you call "silent music," and how silent music is really part of this medicine tradition, and how it informs your work. You've also talked using words like "confirmation" and "intention" as things that are central to the spiritual side of what you do as a musician. Can you elaborate on this in relation to what you've been speaking about in terms of music and its more spiritual dynamics?

IBRAHIM: Let me tell you a story. A few years ago I was in Japan giving concerts and studying with my martial arts teacher. And this man approached me who had been living in Japan and was also involved with the martial arts. He asked me what I knew about Zen. I said, "What do you mean?" He said, "What is Zen?" I said, "It is the first thing that comes into your mind." And he said to me, "That's not true!" [Pause, laughter.] You see, all this is very practical. This is not about reading old esoteric texts. This is very simple stuff and very functional and very direct.

There was this saxophone player I knew early on. And he used to play these harmonics that would go "eeekkk, eeekkk." We used to call them "squeaks." And people who were playing with him would say, "Come on, man! We are playing a ballad!" [Laughs.] Later, I came to the United States at the time of the beginnings of the so-called avant-garde movement in New York. We were playing this music and were technically proficient, you know. I had come here, and there were New Yorkers in my band playing this squeak. And I said, "Wait a minute, man. We are playing music here so that people can dance." [Laughs.]

When I went back to South Africa, I went to see the sax player with the squeak. To tell him about this, you know. I said to him, "Have you heard this avant-garde music?" He said, "Yeah, man. Old stuff." I said, "Yeah, but you've been playing that stuff for a long time. I remember when I first started playing with you." And he said, "Do you remember those dances that we used to play? There was this beautiful woman there and every time that she would walk into the room, that's when I made that sound." That's why he was making those squeaks! [Laughs.] We didn't realize what he was doing. He never mentioned it. So you see, it's all practical. In this case, there was a practical connection with the squeaks to this woman's walking into the room and his reaction to that. And this was part of the history of the beginnings of avant-garde jazz.

This reminds me of another story. The student comes to the teacher and asks, "Teacher, how do we meditate?" And the teacher says, "Keep on meditating." [Laughs.] You see what I'm getting at here?

THOMAS RAIN CROWE: Speaking of meditation, your music reminds me in some ways of that of Charles Lloyd. Do you know Charles Lloyd and his music?

IBRAHIM: Charlie, oh yeah. We knew each other. He lives on the West Coast now, doesn't he? Hasn't he been living out there for years? Yes, I remember his album *Forest Flower*. Yes.

CROWE: He told me some great stories about people you've also known, such as Miles, Coltrane, Monk, Billie Holliday, and Duke Ellington.

IBRAHIM: Back when Coltrane was playing in Miles's band, they used to come through and we'd all get together to talk about things. On one of these trips I was sitting with Miles after a gig. I noticed that during the gig every time that Trane would begin playing one of his solos, Miles would walk off the bandstand and go to the bar. Just leave the stage the whole time Trane was playing. So, I asked him, I said, "Miles, why is it that every time Trane starts in with his solo you go to the bar?" And Miles says, in that deep gravelly voice of his, "It's because he plays his solos too long." About that time Coltrane comes over and sits down, and because we're talking about him, Miles turns to him and says, "Why do you play those long solos, man?" Trane is somewhat taken by surprise, but sort of casually responds by saying, "It's because I'm into it. I can't stop." And Miles says to him right back, "You can't stop? Did you ever try taking the horn out of your mouth?!" [Laughs.]

You know, there was this woman in New York back in those days who was supposed to be channeling Coltrane's solos. She was getting them and writing them down and telling people that Coltrane was giving them to her from another dimension or something. Finally, someone took some of those channeled solos to Coltrane to get him to verify the transcriptions. He looked at them for some time and then said, "I can't play this, it's too difficult!" [Laughs.] So in a sense, he was saying that his so-called own music was too difficult for him to play.

CROWE: There was a piece that you began and ended your set with last night that really struck me. It struck me in a similar way that Charles Lloyd's piece entitled "The Blessing" did on first listen.
IBRAHIM: It must have been "Maraba Blue." [Hums melody.]

CROWE: That's it!
IBRAHIM: Maraba is a township near Pretoria. This is where contemporary South African township music was born. The translation from rural music to urban music actually happened in that part of South Africa, in Maraba. This piece of mine is dedicated to the energy field that has been created out of Maraba. They discovered something there that released us, so it's all in the discovery, isn't it? Self discovery means everything. Because we've been told so many untruths. I think of it as the veil being lifted from ourselves. Maraba.

CROWE: I'd like to pick up on your idea of the "veil" here. A new book of my versions from *The Divan* of the fourteenth-century Persian poet, Hafiz, has just been published. Hafiz alludes in his poetry to the lifting of the veil. The veil being the thing that exists between ourselves and a greater perception of reality. I'm wondering, based on what we've been talking about here, if you are familiar with the Persian poets of Islam—the Sufi poets Hafiz, Rumi, Kabir, and others—and what influence these teachers of Islam may have had on you and your work as a musician and as a practicing Muslim.

IBRAHIM: Yes, we know of these poets. We read Rumi and the others. But beyond that this is a subject that we really don't know too much about.

Let me say this. I don't know what you would call the mindset of jazz musicians. But it's always instructive to tell the stories of certain musicians. Another story about Miles and Monk comes to mind.

Miles got to the point when he was on the cover of *Time* magazine and all this sort of thing, and was setting up recording dates, and one time all the musicians were there, but Monk didn't show up, so finally they had to cancel the session. I think it was the next day and Miles's manager meets Monk on the street. And he asks Monk, "What happened yesterday?" And Monk says, "What are you talking about?" And the manager says, "We were at the recording session and everybody was waiting for you." And Monk says, "I wasn't there?" [Laughs.] Monk was kinda that way. He was something else.

WATKINS: I'd like to move to another subject for a moment and ask you, what was it like for you to return to South Africa after all those years of being away? How was the music scene? And how did it feel for you to return home?

IBRAHIM: So, so traumatic. You have to understand that now we are putting the pieces back together. Regenerating the community. Just learning how to use the space. This now is a vital role. Especially musically. There is a dimension in our culture which was completely eradicated and a lot of people had to go into exile. But there, people [in South Africa] who loved music started up incredible jazz clubs, and they had them all over the country. People would meet informally in the communities at these jazz clubs and exchange records and CDs. Literally hundreds of these jazz clubs all over the country. In some cases these were the centers of community interaction as apartheid was broken.

Just before we came here [to the United States] this time, there was a launch of my new CD in Johannesburg, and it was a most incredible event. We had to turn away about two hundred people and the place was packed. What we did was to provide food, and we played some and the people were there because they loved the music, and because it provided a chance for everyone to get together. So, it was a launch not so much in the sense of launching a CD, but also launching the whole idea of what community has been in our lives. So we've been given the task now to demystify all of those apartheid structures. And it's good. At times it's a lot of hard work. There are many dedicated people. Also what is gratifying is that people in the business sector are drawing us into the businesses, which is helping us to survive the hardships of this transition.

WATKINS: How much time are you actually able to spend in South Africa?
IBRAHIM: I have just come from there and I'll have to be returning in ten days.

WATKINS: Are you doing a lot of commuting these days?
IBRAHIM: These are crucial moments now that we are working to establish these music centers. To open up another part of the bridge for those of us who love the music. We can come to Charleston and we can come to Cape Town.

CROWE: It must have been an amazing time to be there after the release of Mandela and to be witness to how things have been turned around.
IBRAHIM: The president and the people around him, they are remarkable. They are remarkable people. Vision. The vision that

they have. It would have been very easy to have taken South Africa down the road to disaster. It was very scary there just before elections. Those three weeks leading up to the first elections were terrifying. It was almost like people were preparing for a state of war. I remember on the night before the elections, Mandela was on national television. It was incredible. The interviewer was trying to pigeonhole him, but he turned the whole thing around, in the end making the interviewer look stupid, as Mandela laughed saying there was nothing to worry about. The interviewer asked, "Mr. Mandela, have the defense forces been alerted?" And Mandela replied, "We don't need defense forces. The police can handle this." This had the effect of calming the people and giving them a kind of confidence. Mandela knows about everything. He was in prison for twenty-seven years and had a lot of time to think. When you talk to him, you always feel that what you are saying is stupid. But there are tremendous things happening. Some very fine people leading the country now.

WATKINS: Do you know Mandela personally?

IBRAHIM: Yes we do. One time he came to hear us play at one of our concerts. Someone backstage went up to him and asked him what he thought of the music. He said, "Everybody in the West talks about Bach and Beethoven. But we've got better."

WATKINS: Last night while listening to your performance, the word that kept coming to mind was "praise." I'm thinking, too, of "The Praise Song" on your album, *Desert Flowers*. Is there some form of praise tradition in South Africa to which you are connected and which may also inform your music? In the melodies and in the pauses, your whole set seemed like an extended hymn.

IBRAHIM: Yes, there's a tradition of praise singers. They are in all different nations. They are members of the king's court or the chief's court singing praises. Oh, the praise singers, ooooh! They are something else! There is one youngster, I think he must be about eleven or twelve years of age, he is something else. The praise singers, they sing at rallies, sometimes at community meetings, major events. Praise singing is a tradition. For all people. In Islam we have praise for the Prophet. All this helps us to remain positive. We must transcend the blues.

WATKINS: I think of postmodernism as being the opposite of praise. We have a lot of that in our art and music in this country, and it's refreshing to hear the praise.

IBRAHIM: We are both fortunate and unfortunate in our traditions. And this is what we are trying to really capture and salvage from our culture.

WATKINS: I'd like to go back to the subject of so-called spiritual chords or keys that I mentioned earlier. As I say, your music is very uplifting. I'd like to hear a little more about the mechanics of your composing and your musical choices when improvising.

IBRAHIM: In order to hear the music, you first have to hear yourself. Often we are hidden from ourselves. If you don't know what your sound is, you cannot really project your sound. It's always a question of identity. Identifying your own sound. Also, through the process of elimination, one will come to a formula which is most direct. Straight and direct. And when you have uncovered the "why" of all these details, it is the same thing with the harmony.

I'm thinking of the bass players. There is completely another way of thinking. And the guitar players have a hard time playing this music. You cannot just play in the root position; you have first inversion and second inversion of the chord, and unless you play the correct inversion, it doesn't sound right. And the bass player also. If he has something like a B-flat chord, and a particular chord calls for him to play D, instead of B-flat—if he just plays B-flat, he completely destroys the essence of the song. Destroys its sacredness. If there are five notes in the chord, it is not necessary to play all five. It is not necessary. The harmonies are always moving, and sometimes less is more.

CROWE: I think it was in the liner notes to your CD *Yarona* that you said the trio is an essential formula for the pianist/composer. Is that connected to what you are saying here?

IBRAHIM: We are dealing with elements here. The five elements. Water, fire, metal, wood, earth. These are also essential and basic principles of medicine. This is what I mean, in context, by trio being important to the piano. The elements, medicine, music are all connected, and you need all five. All five.

CROWE: I understand that you've made around two hundred recordings. How have you been able to find the time to put out so many albums?

IBRAHIM: We've made so many because we work quickly. A day or two on an album. We have many labels—here and in South Africa, and the Enja label in Germany. We recorded *Desert Flowers*, for example, in one day. Our trio recorded *Yarona* live in two days at Sweet Basil in New York.

WATKINS: Some years ago, I made the transition from piano to synthesizer. I've noticed that on albums such as *Desert Flowers* you, too, have incorporated electronic keyboards into your compositions and arrangements. I find that the electronic instruments are very different, don't you think?

IBRAHIM: Yes. And we use the synthesizer very sparingly. On the other hand, Tsakwe, my son, he's into it with his music. He set up the keyboard program for the album. And my daughter Tsidi is also a musician in a rap group. And, of course, Sathima, my wife, is a singer. We are all musicians.

SATHIMA BEA BENJAMIN

An African Songbird in New York

Following our experiences with Abdullah Ibrahim at the Spoleto USA Festival in the summer of 1998, both Nan Watkins and I were intrigued with the stories we heard from him about his family, and particularly his wife Sathima Bea Benjamin. The story of their association with Duke Ellington particularly got our attention. Abdullah had very generously given us Sathima's contact information in New York and encouraged us to call her. Not being one to pass up such an opportunity, and with our curiosity piqued (neither of us had heard her singing), Nan jumped in to the task of doing some research on her prior to any contact or conversations.

With notes in hand, we made our initial call to Sathima Bea Benjamin that same summer, soon after our time in Charleston, and were able to reach her at her Chelsea Hotel apartment on the first try. Right away Sathima and Nan (both being women and musicians) hit it off. What followed over the next several weeks was a steady stream of phone conversations and letters that included a few of her most recent CDs, not the least of which was the recent release of *A Morning in Paris*, the long-lost recording of her session in Paris with Duke Ellington and Billy Strayhorn back in 1963.

Throughout the fall of that year, there were long listening sessions to the CDs, work on consolidation of the phone conversations, and much research, all of which resulted in a written narrative that was part biographical profile and part interview that would appear as a major feature for *Jazz News* magazine in December 1998 under Nan's byline. In fact, during that period Nan and Sathima had actually spent time together in New York—which included a visit to a small café near the Chelsea—where they had listened to old tapes of Sathima and Billy Strayhorn on Sathima's daughter's Walkman while drinking coffee over a late breakfast.

While Nan was busy writing the narrative for the article in *Jazz News*, I was working on a review of *A Morning in Paris*, which would appear alongside Nan's profile of Sathima in the same issue. Written in an ecstatic voice, it was my intention to introduce not only this landmark, if not historic, recording, but also Sathima Bea Benjamin, the jazz singer, to an expanded American audience.

Here, then, are the fruits of our labors—we three—in the form of three published pieces from that first year that serve as an heraldic invocation of the muse, which in this case is none other than the wonderful voice and phrasing of Sathima Bea Benjamin. The correspondence and friendship between Sathima, Nan, and myself has continued until this day. And although ten years have passed since our first contact and Sathima's sixty-second birthday celebration, she continues to work on new recording projects, and her voice continues to amaze.

Talking by phone with Sathima Bea Benjamin, jazz singer from Cape Town, South Africa, in her adopted home in the Chelsea Hotel in New York City on a late summer evening, I heard stories, so many stories of her life as a jazz singer of multicultural heritage trying to find ways to express her creative gift. "It's a lonely road, that's all I can say. It's a lonely road for jazz singers. You wish you could come out of the loneliness and be like ordinary people. This music has to be your world," she told me as our conversation hit the half-an-hour mark. Her stories tell of the high points—making her first recording with Duke Ellington in Paris in 1963; touring European nightclubs with the Dollar Brand Trio; singing with Ellington's band at the Newport Jazz Festival; founding Ekapa, her own recording label; returning to South Africa to sing at Nelson Mandela's inauguration—and the low points of growing up classified "colored" in apartheid South Africa, of leaving her beloved homeland seeking freedom from racial oppression, of learning that the tapes she laid down with Ellington were somehow lost. Hers is a life of great highs and lows, perceived with sensitivity and humility, and lived from the heart.

Hearing a recording by Sathima Bea Benjamin for the first time is like discovering a shimmering pearl you hadn't noticed before on your favorite stretch of beach. You hear a clear, mellow, slightly melancholy voice so natural and subtle that its beauty floods the room like the first beams of sunlight at dawn. Benjamin has been in love with music since her earliest days of childhood, and now, at age sixty-two, she is determined to finish the work of giving back to others the talent that was given to her as a young girl in Cape Town. "It's a circular process," she says, "giving back what God has given you. You give it away and then you must replenish the gift within you."

"I knew very early that I was extra-ordinary and would have something to give the world. I knew I had been given a special talent to sing—and that I would have to act ordinary if I wanted to interact easily with others. But you can be extra-ordinary when you do your work. When you make music."

Benjamin admits, "Without the music I would be dysfunctional and maybe a bit mad. It was the songs that took me out of myself and let me forget the pain." The pain began as a young girl of four in Cape Town when her parents divorced. "I didn't have a regular childhood," she goes on. "I was not raised by my parents." After the break-up, she was sent to various aunts and her grandmother until her father remarried when she was seven. When she and her younger sister went to live with him, they were forced to endure harsh and abusive treatment from their stepmother. During these years Benjamin began mothering her younger sister, trying to protect her from "the horrendous treatment." By the time she was nine, her grandmother, "very dark, with straight black hair," who had emigrated as a girl from the Isle of St. Helena in the mid-Atlantic to Cape Town, legally adopted her and her younger sister, and they became part of the large household of her grandmother's ten children, several of whom still lived at home. Benjamin says it was her grandmother who gave her the sense of beauty. She remembers her as a loving woman who lived by an old-fashioned strict code of ethics.

In her grandmother's home, Benjamin's lifelong affair with music began. There was an old-fashioned record player, an RCA Victrola, where she heard the old songs like "Sweet Mystery of Life." Her grandmother's friends would stop by on Sunday afternoons and there would be singing from light operettas. She would listen to the popular music on the radio and would take pencil and paper and write down the lyrics. She discovered that she had "a photographic memory for melody" and began singing what she heard. Her grandmother signed her up for piano lessons—just for a year—so that she learned to read a few notes. As she grew older she sang in the choir at the local Anglican church. All of these musical experiences worked like magic for her, allowing her to forget the painful circumstances of growing up: being without her natural parents, and being subjected to the rule of the Afrikaaners, and as a schoolchild required to learn Afrikaans, "the language of the oppressor." (She says today, somewhat proudly, that she speaks Afrikaans very poorly.)

As she grew older and was in high school, she became aware of Cape Town at large. It was a melting pot of various races, and a very musical place. She remembers the hawkers with their horses and carts singing in the streets as they hawked their wares, singing the special folk rhythms of the Cape that she says are still the basis for all her own music.

At home with her grandmother and in her early teens, she found she could not talk about singing a cappella in the local variety shows. The strict atmosphere of the household did not permit that, so she held this musical pleasure within, embracing it as a secretive art. It wasn't until her mid-teens that she moved in with her mother and learned that her mother was naturally musical. She played ragtime by ear on the piano in her home. Her mother bought her a record player and she listened to all the popular songs—not yet jazz—and her friends told her that when she sang she sounded like Doris Day.

When she was still in high school training to be a teacher, she sang in the school choir. After a while she was not content to just sing in the choir, but wanted a solo part. The story has been reported how she asked the choir director, who was directing classical music, why he never asked her to sing a solo, because she knew she had a good voice. He replied, "You are very lucky that I keep you in the choir. I can't ask you to sing a solo because you swoop." The choir director wanted her to hit the note directly instead of sliding into it. Today Benjamin says, "Swooping gave me my direction. My voice does not have vibrato. It is like a saxophone without vibrato. Sometimes I think of my voice as a saxophone. My range and technique are not that powerful so I slide up to a note. I developed this way of singing the songs I love so much. It turns out to be my technique." A technique that the choir director saw as a flaw. But because she sings "from that deep place within" rather than in a contrived or studied manner, she allowed her natural "swooping" to became her trademark.

By age eighteen, the young Bea Benjamin had finished school and began her job teaching children during the week. She was invited to sing in her first jazz concert, enticed by the suggestion that if she would come to the concert, she would be introduced to the local jazz musicians. She went and sang "Don't Blame Me" and she remembers, "The audience went crazy."

That was the beginning of two years of performing gigs every weekend in the local white nightclubs for the white audiences to eat and dance to the music while the black musicians were sent to the kitchen after they performed. She calls those two years "my night school" where she learned all the jazz standards and developed a love of performing them. During this time she tried to find a pianist who would perform with her, but "the guys would always want to be my boyfriend. I was just looking for a pianist." She remembers that after the gigs she would join the guys—she was always the

only girl—and go to one of their houses and listen late into the
night to records of Charlie Parker, Billie Holiday, Stan Getz, and
all the greats. There was a lot of interest at that time in South
Africa in the American jazz scene. It was then that she developed
a liking for Duke Ellington's music and that she began wondering
about the situation of the black jazz artists in the United States as
a parallel to her own situation as a "colored" in South Africa, a
"colored" who had to keep in her restricted place and could not
mix freely with the other races. She recognized a connection with
the American jazz artists who were subjected to racial oppression
in America the way she was subjected to it in South Africa. This
attraction to American jazz has remained throughout her life, liberating her spirit in those early days in South Africa, as it continues
to liberate her spirit today.

One evening in 1959, a Swiss graphic artist was putting on a
big jazz event and needed a singer. "He thought I was the very best
singer that South Africa had." He told her that he had "the most
wonderful pianist" lined up for the concert and that she should
meet him. At the rehearsal, Bea Benjamin met Dollar Brand who
later in the week accompanied her in the concert on the Ellington
tune "I've Got It Bad (and That Ain't Good)." It turned out to be a
fateful meeting for Benjamin. In that one evening she met the man
she would marry, Dollar Brand (later to be known as Abdullah
Ibrahim). The tune that she sang that evening was written by the
man who would bring her to Paris to make her first recording,
Duke Ellington. The Swiss artist who brought Dollar Brand and
Bea Benjamin together, Paul Meyer, was instrumental in bringing
the two to Switzerland three years later when the harsh racial politics of South Africa forced them to leave their homeland.

Describing the days after she met Dollar Brand, Benjamin says,
"I saw [Abdullah] on and off through the week and our relationship developed and before we knew it we were like two peas in a
pod. And then we kind of were together. We did concerts together,
worked together, however we could. It was getting very difficult to
perform in South Africa because of all the new laws. I gave up my

schoolteaching and threw myself into the music. We were literally starving at that point. Paul Meyer, in the meantime, had gone back to Zurich at the end of 1960. He corresponded with us, and he said, 'I think you two guys should try to come out here. I will see what I can do to help you once you get to Europe.' We didn't know anyone in Europe anywhere. He lived in Zurich, and that's why we went to Zurich. That's why we were there one year later [in 1963] when Duke Ellington came along.

"By that time we had negotiated with the owner of the club called the 'Africana,' and he paid the airfare for the bass player and the drummer to come from Cape Town. And they worked it out so that they had a contract for a year to work in that club. I sang whenever I wanted to. I don't think the owner cared whether I sang or not, but I sang to keep in touch with the music. That's when I was working with the [Dollar Brand] Trio. So when I went into the studio for that recording session with Duke, there was some thought. I had a repertoire that I was doing with the Trio. We more or less knew what I could do. We rehearsed a lot. In Zurich we did a lot of wood chipping getting the music tight."

In Zurich, Benjamin and Brand lived as poor artists among the international students there. She says that in a strange way Switzerland was kind to them. The big break for both of them came when Ellington arrived in town to perform with his band, and Benjamin summoned her courage to go backstage (it was Paul Meyer who helped her get backstage) and ask Ellington to come listen to the music of the Dollar Brand Trio after his show. So around midnight, Ellington accompanied Benjamin through the snowy streets of Zurich to the Club Africana where he listened to the Dollar Brand Trio play after hours. When they had finished, Ellington asked Benjamin, "Are you the manager?" "No," she replied. "But I sing sometimes." "Then you must sing," Ellington said matter-of-factly.

This spontaneous meeting resulted in Ellington giving train tickets to all the musicians so that they could appear in Paris on February 23, 1963, at the Barclay Studios for recording sessions. It was the first time Benjamin ever recorded. Benjamin tells her side of the story: "Ellington was in the booth because he produced the thing. It took us about three hours, that whole CD. I sang about twelve or thirteen songs. He kept saying, 'What are you going to sing next, my darling?' That's what he said. Then Abdullah was playing 'I Got It Bad,' and he came out of the booth and he said, 'Oh, no, that's my song.' And then he sat down at the piano. Can you believe that? I thought, 'Oh, my God!' Duke Ellington was looking at me, and we had a soundproof glass partition so I could see him. And then after we did that song, he said to me, 'Do you know "Solitude?"' And, you know, I had never sung it in my life before. I said, 'Sir,' because I was so shy, 'I know the melody, but I don't know the lyrics.' And he said, 'Somebody write the lyrics for her.' And he taped them up on the glass partition. And he said, 'Well, you know the melody, then we don't have a problem. Take a look at the lyrics, okay?' And he was busy fiddling for a key. And then we found a key and he said, 'Remember what I told you? One take.' But I think we had to do two takes or even three takes, not because of me, but because the bass player wasn't playing what he wanted him to play. He would stop and say, 'No, no, no, no. That's not what I hear.' But that was good because it gave me a chance to look at the lyrics while he was busy with them. And that was the first time in my life that I ever sang 'Solitude.'"

Though the album *Duke Ellington Presents the Dollar Brand Trio*, recorded right after Benjamin sang her dozen songs, appeared within the year, the session of Benjamin's songs was not released, and over time the tapes were lost. This was understandably an enormous disappointment for her, but it turned out that the generosity of Ellington was to help Benjamin and Ibrahim in numerous ways.

When Benjamin was still touring Europe singing with the Dollar Brand Trio, in 1965 Ellington contacted them in London and asked them to perform that summer at the Newport Jazz Festival. Benjamin was twenty-eight then. Now she remembers: "We got there at the Festival site in the evening and Duke was due to go on at 10:00 o'clock. He arrived about quarter to ten and I was trying to think, 'What am I going to sing?' I was so nervous. And Duke said, 'Oh, what are you nervous about? You go stand on the side of the stage and when I introduce you, then you come on, okay?' That's how he would empower you. And then when he did introduce me and I walked on, he said, 'How about "Solitude?"' And he said, 'What key?' And luckily I remembered the key. That's how Duke Ellington got anything out of you. If Duke Ellington told you you were going to do it, then you did it. And if anybody else would tell you to do the same thing, you would say, 'You have to be crazy. I can't do that.'

"So we began 'Solitude,' and then I heard the band playing with me and I couldn't believe it! Can you imagine how awesome that was? When I heard that band playing behind me, I didn't care if I sang again for the rest of my life." Benjamin goes on to describe the unique qualities of Ellington: "He taught me that you've got to have the element of spontaneity. He also taught me to have faith in my work. Ellington was such a force. I think he must have been very clairvoyant and quite a psychologist, and I think that's how he kept that band together. Because everyone, whenever they played their solos, they excelled! He injected something in you with his gaze and the way he would tell you to do something. I was absolutely in awe of the man. Duke Ellington was utterly charming and gentlemanly. I've never met another man like that in my life and I don't think I ever will. He was the ultimate gentleman."

It was toward the end of the sixties when Benjamin and Ibrahim were living in Brooklyn, that she was given the name "Sathima." It came as a gift from a fellow musician from South Africa whom she had helped through difficult times. After he left New York, he said he would always call her "Sathima," which meant "someone with a kind heart" in his native tongue. Benjamin accepted the name and has used it ever since as her own. By chance, several years later she met an elderly Indian gentleman in the African National Congress headquarters in New York. He asked about her name and told her that "Sathima" was an ancient Sanskrit word meaning "God's truth."

By 1970 Benjamin and Ibrahim returned to South Africa, opening the Marimba School of Music in Mbabane, Swaziland. Sathima gave birth to their son, Tsakwe, in Cape Town, an act that was deliberately planned to take place in their native South Africa. In 1972 they were back in Denmark touring with the group, Music of Universal Silence, founded by Ibrahim and Don Cherry. Christmas Eve, 1972, found Benjamin singing in the Jazz Vespers with Duke Ellington at St. Peter's in New York.

In 1976 they again returned to South Africa, this time for the birth of their daughter, Tsidi. It was not long after that when Benjamin gathered together some local musicians and made the first recording of her own work, *African Songbird*, on the Sun label. She comments that her own songs were so spacious that she couldn't write them down. Instead of using standard instrumentation, she got a recording of seagulls and sang the title song against the soundscape of seagull cries. She was not to remain long in South Africa; the racial violence worsened, and after the tragedy of the Soweto riots, Benjamin and Ibrahim once again left their homeland and returned to New York, this time in self-exile.

By now Benjamin had two young children to raise while her husband was more often than not on the road pursuing his career as an international jazz artist. After years of being on the road herself, she longed for stability and a place to bring up her children. So she settled the family in New York at the Chelsea Hotel, which she has called home ever since.

Before long, she began missing her music. What should she do if she wasn't performing on tour? She had heard about Betty Carter founding her own recording company back in the sixties and decided to try the same herself. It was a brave step, for as she admits, "I knew nothing about recording and was stupid about business." But she persevered. She called a musician friend of Ibrahim's and asked him to recommend some musicians she could work with. He suggested Vishnu Wood on bass, Onaje Allan Gumbs on piano, and John Betsch on drums. No one knew her, she says, and she seems surprised that they would have agreed to work with her. They rehearsed, she engaged Downtown Sound Studios, and one night in April 1979 they recorded *Sathima Sings Ellington*. She writes on the liner notes, "The recording session which started around midnight and ended up in the early hours of the morning was extremely relaxed and enjoyable. Please do not think me presumptuous when I say that there were moments during the session when I felt 'his' spirit very strongly—and that was beautiful."

This, her debut album in the United States, is inscribed: "To DUKE ELLINGTON from AFRICA with LOVE, "SATHIMA BEA BENJAMIN." No longer available, the album is a treasure of sophisticated Ellington songs—including "Lush Life" by Billy Strayhorn—sung by one of the few living jazz vocalists who worked with Ellington. The tenderness of the vocal line in "Solitude" is so fragile as to nearly break. The version on this album includes only drums as accompaniment—no piano—because Benjamin forever holds sacred Duke Ellington's accompaniment in her head from that morning in Paris, in February 1963, when he asked her to sing it for his Reprise label.

So, having recorded the music for her first independently produced album, she was then faced with finding a factory to make the master, producing the records, and preparing the photo and liner notes for the album cover. Ibrahim produced the album, and her new label Ekapa (The Cape) was born. When she finally had the finished product, the next question was what to do with all those records. She mailed albums to twenty-some critics, and again seemed surprised that they liked it and recommended it. Distributors even began calling her.

The eighties turned out to be a productive time for Benjamin. "I wanted to be stationary. I wanted to be with my children because their dad was hardly ever here. He was the breadwinner. So we really have to thank him because he was very generous. He was performing and making record after record." Benjamin herself continued to record more albums on her Ekapa label, and many of the works were her own compositions. *Dedications* followed in 1982, again financed by their own income and produced by Ibrahim. By this time she was working with "the masters" Buster Williams on bass, Ben Riley on drums, and Onaje Allan Gumbs still on piano and the arranger of all the numbers on the album. She says she has "a bond with these three." Dom Um Ramao makes a guest appearance on percussion, as does Carlos Ward on flute. "I think I've been blessed in finding people or being led to people or just knowing who to go to and say, 'I want to work with you,'" Sathima says about her collaborators.

Two of Benjamin's own songs appear on *Dedications*: "Music" and "Africa." Both songs she wrote in South Africa in 1974 and premiered in Carnegie Hall in June 1981. They announce the haunting voice of the African Songbird in New York. In "Music" she sings: "Music is the spirit deep within you. Find yourself, then let it flow. Find your sound, then let it flow. Sweet and easy. And go." "Africa" is an extraordinary rendering of the African sensibility in the exquisite intonation of the word, "Africa." It is clear that, living in New York, she longs for the spirit of her native Africa. "Cooperation is a very African thing. I think that's a very African outlook [as opposed to competition]. Our kind of humility is not really understood here. People here think that if you are humble, then you are some kind of a sucker. Some kind of fool. It's not that way where I come from."

On October 7, 1983, Benjamin was back in the studio, this time with Rudy Van Gelder as recording engineer and joined again by Gumbs, Williams, Riley, and Ward, and another "master," Billy Higgins on drums, for her own composition on the album *Memories and Dreams*. Side one was taken up by Benjamin's major work, "Liberation Suite," consisting of "Nations in Me—New Nation A'Coming," "Children of Soweto," and "Africa." "Nations in Me," as Benjamin says, is really three songs in one. Laced with sparkling work by Ward and Gumbs on flute and piano, the song begins with Benjamin's sure, clear voice describing her multiracial South African heritage, then stating the cold facts of apartheid society, and finally moving with resolute grace directly into "A New Nation A'Coming":

Nations in me
I have so many nations in me.
Looking at my family tree
I believe that I'm the fruit of their love.
In the land of my birth
You're told you're of no worth
If you're black or have nations in you
So much humiliation and pain
But we know it's their loss and our gain
For our struggle will not be in vain.
For there's a new nation a'coming
There'll be no talk about color
We won't be concerned about race
For we're building a new nation
With just one beautiful face.

Speaking of her multicultural background, Sathima Benjamin says, "I can't claim one nationality. I will always be an outsider, because I don't fit into any one compartment. There is no compartment for me. I am so multiracial I cannot decipher it. It can be very painful. But I am the sum of all those genes and I am very proud to say that."

She tells of her first real sense that freedom would some day arrive in South Africa and how this inspired the writing of "New Nation A'Coming." "We had attended the independence celebrations in Maputo, Mozambique. It was wonderful, liberating, mind-boggling. You could feel the warmth, the tenderness. I thought, this is how it will be. One day South Africa will be free. On the way back in the plane—it was a long journey—I wrote that song, 'New Nation A'Coming.'" A number of years later, in 1994, Benjamin found herself celebrating the liberation of her own country by singing a solo, "Come Sunday," at Nelson Mandela's inauguration as President of South Africa.

The debut of her "Liberation Suite" was hailed by the *Philadelphia Tribune*: "Ms. Benjamin's technique is awesome. On her suite, she at times captures the sound of gospel (or gospel's African precursor?), a Coltrane horn, or the hollow timbre of an African flute. Each word is invested with emotion, and the sliding of a note or tremolo as a syllable cascades leaves the listener shaken."

In sum, Benjamin has released seven Ekapa albums. *WindSong* was recorded in 1985 by Rudy Van Gelder and produced by Ibrahim. Kenny Barron on piano joins Williams on bass and Higgins on drums playing all of Benjamin's arrangements, ranging from her tender version of "Sometimes I Feel Like a Motherless Child," which she traditionally opens her performances with, to Victor Herbert's "Indian Summer" and three of her own songs: "WindSong," "Lady Day," and "Dreams." She says of "Lady Day": "The song came around midnight, and I wasn't even thinking about it. The whole thing came within a half an hour. It's very scary. I couldn't sleep the whole night. The next morning I had to rush to the studio where I usually do my rehearsing, because I knew this guy had a tape recorder and I couldn't get hold of Buster Williams or anyone. So I said to him, 'If I sing this, could you just write it down?'" Again, the music had come full circle. Benjamin recalls, "When I first heard Billie Holiday, she made me feel okay. I said to myself, 'It's okay to sing like this. To put it from the soul. Every word.'"

She remembers the composition of "WindSong" as a kind of identity crisis. She was in South Africa, "personally in a desert with myself. 'WindSong' came—I just heard a bass line—I didn't hear any melody—I just heard that gorgeous bass line—and it wouldn't go away. It stayed, as if it were being played in my head, then gradually the rhythm, lines of movement, then lyrics and melody. They come together when they have to come together, you know. It was spacious and wide. And then I thought, 'What kind of a song is this?' I was terribly shy about presenting it. The first one I went to was Abdullah—he and I had been apart for about a year and a half and then I met up with him again. I asked him, and it was then that I found out that what I was writing was really a song."

Attempting to describe how the music comes to her, Benjamin says, "The music has to speak. It comes from a very faraway place.

One has this humility. I think that what God gives, he can also take away. You have to be very careful what you do with your gift. I can't say that strongly enough. You have to be very careful how you mold it. You can't keep it to yourself. You have to give it away so that you can refill. And so you have to trust that God is going to keep giving it to you. I've just had this approach. And it's natural, completely natural, and it works. It allows for a lot of love and a lot of tenderness to flow in between. It's a kind of purity."

Benjamin closed out the eighties by recording *Lovelight* in 1987 and *Southern Touch* in 1989. Both CDs were released by Matthias Winckelmann on the Enja label of Munich in the early nineties. They are collections of popular songs including Ellington, Strayhorn, Kern, and Coward, along with a few of her own songs. Backed by her master musicians, Benjamin's voice still sings out the great songs like "I Let a Song Go Out of My Heart" with an energy and clarity that continue to delight all who hear them.

In addition to singing at Mandela's inauguration, the high point of the nineties for Benjamin has to be the release of *A Morning in Paris*, the album she recorded when she was twenty-six with Ellington in Paris in 1963. The copy of the duplicate tape made secretly by the recording engineer, Gerhard Lehner, came to light, and the would-be Reprise recording was released by Enja. Benjamin celebrated the event by giving a performance in Weill Recital Hall of Carnegie Hall on February 23, 1997, thirty-four years to the day since the Ellington recording session. It's hard to imagine the thoughts that went through her head that day. The *Village Voice* said of the new release of the singer's first recording: "Benjamin's singing is fascinating, even haunting. . . . When she holds long notes, coloring each line with her distinctively African intonation, . . . the effect is mesmerizing."

Though Benjamin loves New York City "because there's a great electric current that runs through this place and helps me stay creative," she admits today to a desire to return to South Africa. "It's not easy," she says, "because my two children are really New Yorkers and my husband wants to be in South Africa all the time."

She concludes, "It will happen when it should happen." In 2006, in a special ceremony in Johannesburg, Sathima Bea Benjamin was given the Ecamanga Award of Excellence for her lifetime contribution to the music and culture of South Africa.

As for the future, Benjamin says, "I have lots of things I want to do. I want to record a *Sathima Sings Strayhorn* album. And I want to do a CD that's going on in my mind of the songs I heard in Cape Town growing up. Not folk songs, but the songs I heard on the radio, all those beautiful old tender songs. It's important I get to the studio and make as many CDs as I possibly can. And that God spares me enough time on this earth so that I can do it.

"Going into the studio is what I love most. If I never had to perform again, it wouldn't bother me at all. I come out of myself in the studio. I have the guys who are masters at what they do, and the best engineers. I try to remember what Duke Ellington said about doing one take. If there's a technical hitch, okay, two takes. But for heaven's sakes, don't do three takes because you will sound like a very bad imitation of yourself. I'll go into the studio and I'll be out of there in four hours. It's actually very spiritual. A spiritual moment when you connect."

Ending our long conversation together, Benjamin concludes, "My music speaks of hope. It is uplifting music because it comes from that faraway place deep within. It comes from the heart. Never be afraid to research that place within. Don't be afraid to go inside yourself. It is empowering for your art form. Then you can be as unique as you truly are."

A Morning in Paris Sathima Bea Benjamin (Enja Records, 1997)

[This review by Thomas Rain Crowe appeared in *Jazz News*, December 1998]

In the *Philadelphia Tribune* in 1983, columnist Jules Epstein wrote of jazz singer Sathima Bea Benjamin, "There may be ten great jazz singers alive today. Sathima Bea Benjamin is unquestionably one." Whether or not one accepts this kind of adulation by jazz critic Jules Epstein as fact, Sathima Bea Benjamin has to be the jazz world's best kept secret. And the release this past year of her first solo recording *A Morning in Paris* (Enja Records), as well as being something of a Cinderella story, is strange proof.

In February of 1963, Duke Ellington heard a twenty-seven-year-old Bea Benjamin sing at the Club Africana in Zurich, Switzerland. The next day she was invited to the Barclay Studios in Paris for an impromptu recording session with musicians Billy Strayhorn, Svend Asmussen, Johnny Gertze, Makayo Ntshoko, Dollar Brand (Abdullah Ibrahim), and the Duke himself. A one-take taped session was completed that same day with twelve songs featuring Bea Benjamin vocals. With Ellington and Strayhorn on pianos, this recording had enormous potential to launch Bea Benjamin into international prominence.

Unluckily, the people at Reprise Records (Ellington's label at the time) felt that the Bea Benjamin session wasn't commercial and so killed the project for production. If that wasn't enough, she was told that the masters for the taped session had been lost. Bea Benjamin had never even heard the taped session which she had done with Ellington. But this is not the end of the story. . . . Thirty years later, in 1994 destiny stepped in and through a minor miracle Sathima Bea Benjamin got her first chance to listen to the Ellington/Strayhorn tape that had been discovered by Gerhard Lehner, the engineering supervisor for the 1963 session. The lost tape had miraculously been found and work toward producing the recording that was to launch her career thirty years earlier was begun anew.

In the liner notes for the lost sessions CD *A Morning in Paris* that was finally released by Enja Records late in 1997, Gerhard Lehner wrote the following account of his impressions of that eventful day in Paris in 1963, painting a picture that, itself, serves as a fitting "review" of this amazing (first) new release by Bea Benjamin: "As we began to balance the first theme, I was instantly fascinated by this South African singer who had fled from apartheid—not only was I taken by her exceptional beauty but most of all by her extraordinary subtle voice. The lyrics of the ballads on her album's repertory were simply sublime, outstanding. The soft lighting in the studio, the attentiveness of Duke Ellington and Billy Strayhorn in the booth (and sometimes on the piano), the delicate pizzicati of violinist Svend Asmussen, the generous chords of Dollar Brand, all combined to create a magical atmosphere."

Despite the setback in 1963 of the lost opportunity (and in fact the lost tapes from the session), Bea Benjamin went on to tour with Dollar Brand (Abdullah Ibrahim), Hugh Masekela, and the Jazz Epistles, toured Europe with the Dollar Brand Trio, and was introduced at the Newport Jazz Festival in 1965 by Duke Ellington. That same year she gave concerts at Carnegie Hall in New York and toured the U.S. and South Africa. In 1970 she and Abdullah Ibrahim founded the Marimba School of Music in Swaziland. In 1976 she gave her first tribute to Ellington at the Ellington residence on Riverside Drive in New York City. And in 1979 she recorded on her own record label Ekapa *Sathima Sings Ellington*.

Devoting her time to raising her family during the 1980s, she did little public performing but was able to record three albums during this time—*Dedications*, *Memories and Dreams*, and *WindSong*. In the nineties she has kept up with her passion for working in the studio with Ekapa releases such as *LoveLight* and *Southern Touch*, all of which are prototypical of that morning in Paris in 1963 and the "sublime" and erotically sonorous twenty-seven-year-old voice which is amazingly still intact even after all these years.

Ironically and somewhat anachronistically, today, at age sixty-two, and with the release of *A Morning in Paris*, Sathima Bea Benjamin is at the height of her career. *Jazz Magazine, Paris* has honored *A Morning in Paris* as "CD of the Year" and *City Press* in Johannesburg has recently written, "It is evident that Bea Benjamin is one of the greatest jazz vocalists in the world." And I agree! Even thirty-five years later, Bea Benjamin is as good as any living artist today. So with high praise from abroad, it is time for Sathima Bea Benjamin to become the household name of which she is deserving here in America. *A Morning in Paris* is the vehicle that, with a little help, will get her there. Only the absence of a major record label contract stands in the way of Bea Benjamin's long-overdue rise to jazz-world stardom and immortality.

Sounding like a cross-pollination of the lyrical qualities of the blues-inspired tone of Billie Holiday and the professionalism and projection of Dinah Washington, on *A Morning in Paris* Bea Benjamin is like no other jazz singer I know. With a voice so fluid as to be something akin to a siren's song when heard, she does "The Man I Love" and "Lover Man" on this recording so sensually that Lady Day, I think, would have been taken aback. Then, there are the Ellington and the Strayhorn pieces—"I Got It Bad (and That Ain't Good)," "Solitude," and "Your Love Has Faded"—which she does to near perfection, mirroring the compositional lines and licks of Johnny Gertze on bass and Makaya Ntshoko on drums and Ellington and Strayhorn themselves on piano with digital, yet natural accuracy.

As someone with tremendous loyalties as well as discriminating taste, Bea Benjamin has stuck close to her early mentors Strayhorn and Ellington with regard to song selections she has chosen to sing on her many releases over the years, as well as to record the classic standards from such songwriters as Hammerstein, Noel Coward, Jerome Kern, Gershwin, and Rodgers and Hart. And while she has continually done some of the best arrangements and versions of these great standards, it is with her own original compositions that Bea Benjamin truly stands up to be counted. With her "Liberation Suite" from the album *Memories and Dreams*, which was composed in the 1980s during the time of her affiliation with the African National Congress (ANC) and the liberation struggle in South Africa, she places herself alongside such composer/singers as Abbey Lincoln who have used their music to respond and react to the social issues of their day. With driving and modern up-tempo African and Caribbean rhythms the songs in "Liberation Suite" ("Nations in Me–New Nation a-Coming," "Children of Soweto," and "Africa") liberate Bea Benjamin, the singer, from the ranks of accomplished cover artist to the loftier plateau of songwriter/composer/artist. And she is comfortable and consistent here on recent albums mixing her own compositions in with those of other renowned lyricists and musicians with songs like "Music," "Gift of Love," "Lady Day," "African Songbird," and "Winnie Mandela"—all of which are simple and yet a more energetically sensuous Sathima.

Although her career as a jazz musician began professionally in 1959 in Cape Town, South Africa, when she was with the Harold Jephtah Quartet, her larger career, I believe, began spiritually with the recording session in 1963 on that "morning in Paris."

Now, finally, we are able to be witness to this new beginning, this reincarnation—the rocket that would have launched Bea Benjamin into the upper stratosphere of the international jazz world, then, and has only now been ignited and we are blissfully blinded by the flame.

Cape Town Love, Sathima Bea Benjamin (Ekapa Records, 1999)

[This review by Thomas Rain Crowe appeared in *Jazz News*, September 1999]

If jazz singer Bea Benjamin had spent her whole life and made her career exclusively in her native South Africa, she'd be a big star. This thought keeps repeating itself in my mind as I listen for the first time to Sathima Bea Benjamin's new CD, *Cape Town Love*, from Ekapa Records.

Here in the U.S. where she has spent the last twenty-three years, she is little known, having lived in the shadow of her internationally famous husband Abdullah Ibrahim. How can this be, I ask myself—with her heartfelt and soulful voice and playing and recording with some of the best sidemen in the business (specifically Buster Williams, Billy Higgins, Kenny Barron, and Ben Riley)? Her 1997 Enja release, *A Morning in Paris*, which was actually recorded in 1963 in Paris with Duke Ellington and Billy Strayhorn and then lost for thirty years, was greeted in France with the "Album of the

Year" award—and rightly so. But here in the U.S., a strange relative silence was the cool greeting this album received.

Sathima is like no other jazz singer I know. Her slow, sliding transitions and her cool, understated arrangements of some of the jazz world's most classic standards have given them new life. In my opinion, no one since Holiday has given so much heart and soul to jazz songs, jazz singing. Why is she not a star? The question won't go away.

In *Cape Town Love*, Bea Benjamin has gone back home to Cape Town, South Africa, and recorded some of the songs she heard there at the time when she first began singing. She has searched for and found musicians (keyboardist Henry February, bassist Basil Moses, and drummer Vincent Pavitt) whom she grew up listening to and singing with in her early days to try and recreate the sentiments and flavors of those older standards as she remembered them. Now, forty years later, she brings them back to us with all the youth and newness that she must have sung them then. How can this be true? But it is. At sixty-two she sounds almost like a carbon copy of a twenty-six-year-old Bea Benjamin we hear on *A Morning in Paris*.

If you think that *Kind of Blue* is cool . . . then you ain't heard nothing yet. *Cape Town Love* is not only cool, it's ice. Hot ice. The kind that gives off smoke. With selections like "I'll Be Seeing You," "If I Should Fall in Love Again," and "I Only Have Eyes For You," Sathima takes us back—way back. And the ride down memory lane was never sweeter, never more familiar. Her voice (in a one-take, two-day session), with February's mature stylistic piano phrasing, Moses's impeccable rhythmic sensibility, and Pavitt's synchronistic time-keeping, is like time standing still.

With *Cape Town Love*, Sathima Bea Benjamin has closed an important circle in her life. As she says: "It was an exhilaration and thrilling experience. I do believe we have something beautiful here. There is still so much love coming through our sound and approach to jazz. I dedicate this work to my ancestors, and to Cape Town, the place of my birth and upbringing, and all my fondest musical memories."

STEVE REICH

Taking a Different Train

In May 1998, my Spoleto partner Nan Watkins and I again set out for Charleston, South Carolina. On this trip, one of our goals was to get an interview with new music composer Steve Reich and to see a preview of his new multimedia work titled *Three Tales*. A "musical documentary," as he would refer to it during our interview, *Three Tales* focuses on three events in the twentieth century that had a major impact on human civilization and the future. This historical, high-tech performance would use voice, music, and visual effects, making it a kind of "new opera." In anticipation of our time at Spoleto and in talking with Steve Reich, we entered the city limits of Charleston full of enthusiasm and high expectations.

During the subsequent three days and two nights, we did, indeed, get our interview in a quiet corner of the crowded lobby of one of the finest festival hotels. After seeing the evening production of *Three Tales*, which included, in addition, intense performances of two of Reich's signature pieces, "Different Trains" and "Drumming," we made our notes at a local bistro—preparing for the interview the next morning. Little did we know our conversation would cover the gamut of Reich's passions from the medieval canon to Coltrane, from the music of speech to African drumming.

Born in New York and raised there and in California, Steve Reich graduated with honors in philosophy from Cornell University in 1957. For the next two years, he studied composition with Hall Overton, and from 1958 to 1961 he studied at the Juilliard School of Music with William Bergsma and Vincent Persichetti. He received his M.A. in Music from Mills College in 1963, where he worked with Luciano Berio and Darius Milhaud.

Seeking to delve deeper into the complex rhythms of African music, Reich studied drumming, during the summer of 1970, at the Institute for African Studies at the University of Ghana in Accra. In 1973 and 1974 he studied Balinese Gamelan Semar Pegulingan and Gamelan Gambang at the American Society of Eastern Arts in Seattle and Berkeley, California. From 1976 to 1977 he studied the traditional forms of cantillation (chanting) of the Hebrew scriptures in New York and Jerusalem.

In 1966 Reich founded his own ensemble of three musicians, which rapidly grew to eighteen members or more. Since 1971, Steve Reich & Musicians have frequently toured the world and have the distinction of performing to sold-out houses at venues as diverse as Carnegie Hall and the Bottom Line Cabaret.

Reich's 1988 piece, "Different Trains," marked a new compositional method, rooted in "It's Gonna Rain" and "Come Out," in which speech recordings generate the musical material for musical instruments. The *New York Times* hailed "Different Trains" as a "work of such astonishing originality that breakthrough seems the only possible description . . . it possesses an absolutely harrowing emotional impact." In 1990 Reich received a Grammy Award for Best Contemporary Composition for "Different Trains" as recorded by the Kronos Quartet on the Nonesuch label. In 2006 Nonesuch issued the second boxed set of five CDs of Reich's music, making him one of the most recorded living musicians.

There was considerable buzz about the new Reich/Korot collaboration featured at the 1998 Spoleto USA Festival. It was an in-progress version of *Three Tales*, the second collaboration of Steve Reich and Beryl Korot, and concerned three pivotal events that reflected upon the growth and implications of technology in the twentieth century: "Hindenburg," on the crash of the German zeppelin in New Jersey in 1937; "Bikini," on the atom bomb tests at Bikini atoll from 1946 to 1954; and "Dolly," the sheep cloned in 1997, on the issues of genetic engineering and robotics. Musicians and singers took their places on stage along with a large screen where videotape projections created on computers were shown, presenting the debate about the physical, ethical, and religious nature of technological development. Later, in 2002, *Three Tales* was premiered, entire and in finished form, at the Vienna Festival.

Mid-morning the next day, we made our way over to the hotel, where we met a fully caffeinated Steve Reich with his collaborator and technical partner Beryl Korot. Finding a comfortable nook in the hotel lobby, and after dispensing with the usual awkward introductions and prerequisite chit-chat, we got down to the meat of our meeting: our planned questions and Reich's rapid-fire responses. Happily, Reich was in a talkative, if not jovial, mood, following the success of the previous night's performance and a couple of rave reviews in the local papers. This time the questions for the "conversations with music legends" book would be coming from two directions—from the perspective of a classically trained pianist and an internationally published poet. We had the music and the spoken-word and text angles covered. Or so we thought. . . .

THOMAS RAIN CROWE: I'd like to start with some questions relating to the field of jazz music and possible influences of that tradition on your own music. Billy Taylor, for one, has referred to jazz as "America's classical music." I know, for instance, that you have collaborated with jazz artists such as Pat Metheny in the past. I'm wondering how, as a classically trained and educated musician, you see your musical vision dovetailing with mainstream or avant-garde jazz.

STEVE REICH: By the time I was fourteen I had heard Miles Davis, Kenny Clarke, and Charlie Parker, and I wanted to *be* Kenny Clarke. So I started studying snare drum with a man who eventually became the timpanist for the New York Philharmonic. From the age of fourteen to seventeen or eighteen I tried to play with local bands, playing jazz drums and listening constantly to Miles Davis and a lot of other people. And then probably most importantly, in terms of where I ended up, I must have heard John Coltrane play forty or fifty times live while I was at Juilliard and later while I was at Mills College out on the West Coast. This is when Coltrane was in the "modal jazz" period with Elvin Jones and Jimmy Harrison and McCoy Tyner. And once I heard him play live with Eric Dolphy, which was fantastic. Actually, it was with Wes Montgomery and Eric Dolphy. They played at the Monterey Jazz Festival and they came to the San Francisco Jazz Workshop afterwards and played a couple of sets. This made an enormous impression on me. Here was a man who was playing like an African! I know that, at the time, Terry Riley was also into Coltrane. Coltrane was sort of a musical hero for a lot of us.

I don't think I would have written anything the way I have written it, going all the way back to "Drumming," if it weren't for people like Kenny Clarke, Miles Davis, and John Coltrane, in particular. That's really the most important part of it in terms of the influence of jazz on my own work.

The thing with Pat Metheny happened later. A number of classical guitar players were coming to me and saying, "Your stuff would really be good on plucked strings." And then I was talking to the head of ECM Records. I remember telling him, "A lot of guitarists have been asking me to write for classical guitar. You know, electric guitar is the guitar of our time." To which he replied, "Why don't you do something with Pat Metheny?" [Joel] Horowitz had been with ECM when Pat was still there. It turned out that Pat and I were working with ECM at the same time. So, I said, "Gee, do you think he might be interested?" And he said, "I don't know, but I'll give him a ring." And so, five minutes later I was talking on the phone to Metheny. He said, "Oh yeah, that would be great." I said, "I know how a guitar is tuned, and that's about it." I suggested that we get together so he could show me a few things. And I said to him: "You're going to play this piece, then pretty much after that it's going to be classical players playing this, so I want to write it for them because they use finger technique and pluck the strings." Then he said, "Write single lines. Because that way, whether you are a jazz player or a classical player, you'll be able to do it. You've got all the lines and you'll have all the harmonies anyway. The only chords I use are very, very simple."

CROWE: So, how do these stories, then, tie into the question of how your music, with its classical origins and influences, dovetail with the jazz medium?

REICH: Well, basically, if you think back to the classical music that you and I love, for me it's Bach and Kurt Weill and Ravel. In each one of these great composers you get a taste of their times and their cultures. They weren't necessarily trying to compose historically, but were just trying to give honest expression to the times, in the Europe they were living in. I, on the other hand, grew up in America—in the late 1950s and early sixties. One day I was sitting in Birdland when I was fourteen listening to Kenny Clarke. And what seemed like the next day, in 1974, in London, after a concert in Queen Elizabeth Hall, a guy in long hair and lipstick came up to me and introduced himself by saying "How do you do, I'm Brian Eno." These occurrences are a kind of poetic justice, and occur across time. Or, rather with no regard to time. In my mind, that's the way the world's supposed to be!

When I went to music school, at Juilliard and Mills College, the music of Schoenberg and Boulez is what was ruling the roost. You had to do that, at that time, if you wanted to be taken seriously. I learned how to do this, of course, but it wasn't me. There was a wall in those days between classical music and street music, i.e., jazz, rock, and alternative—or what would later be known as "New Music." One of the things that I'm pleased about in terms of what I've done, is that myself and others, such as La Monte Young, have been able to tear that wall down. And we didn't do this by aiming to bring it down, but rather by just being who we were.

CROWE: That said, would you necessarily draw any connections or similarities to what you are doing and mainstream Jazz? At least in terms of improvisation—

REICH: No, not really. Early on I worked with Ornette Coleman and people like that—who were doing the twelve-tone pieces, you know, that were so popular at the time. But, I have to tell you, they were awful. These pieces. These folks were very self-consciously trying to bring jazz and classical music together. But, eventually, they, too, concluded that the twelve-tone licks just don't make it. In the end, I was a drummer, and I just started doing what came naturally. The jazz influence was there, but it was there without having to put it on the paper, or on the table, so to speak. In my subconscious, I was trying, unconsciously, to come up with some kind of hybrid form of music.

CROWE: Personally, I'm interested in what you've been doing over the years with textual material and spoken word. Like what you've done with William Carlos Williams's work, your desert pieces, and these sorts of things. How important have these kinds of collaborations been to you? And I'm wondering why you've chosen to include spoken lyrics rather than sung lyrics in your compositions.
REICH: That's a big one. The very first pieces of mine that came to public attention included "Come Out." Have you heard that one?

CROWE: No, but I have heard "It's Gonna Rain."
REICH: Yes, this was the first piece I did in this style. Essentially, it is a snippet of a black Pentecostal preacher that I recorded in Union Square in San Francisco, who is talking about Noah and the biblical flood. It's in $F_\#$, which was how I heard his voice, musically, that day. When I used the repetition of his voice, the music of his speech became overpowering. Pentecostal preachers often hover around that area that is between speaking and singing. Children do this, too—especially when they are whining. "Daaaddyyy . . . I waann-naaaannn iicce creeemmm." You've heard this, I'm sure. Children don't have much control over their larynx, which allows for a lot of fluid sound variation in their voices. Both examples, here, are examples of how the human voice can be very melodic.

Specifically, Williams, as an American poet, said that his inspiration for the way he wrote was based on the speech he heard walking in the streets of Paterson, New Jersey, where he lived and worked. This was the source that was feeding him. American speech.

Then, lo and behold, here comes Gary Snyder, Robert Creeley, Allen Ginsberg, and Charles Olson and a whole new generation of poets that we all now know and love that come out of the influence of W. C. Williams. I love Williams's poetry.

Listening to Williams reciting his poems, I realized I was hearing the cadences of his voice: 1-2-3, 1-2-3, 1-2-3 . . . and so forth. His vocal cadences were what he called "the flexible foot"—which is a nonmathematical grouping. A grouping that is identified by ear according to certain stresses and tones. So, this awareness is what brought on my musical compositions using Williams's poems.

Around this same time, I was offered, by the Frankfurt Opera in Frankfurt, Germany, to write an opera. I figured this would take me about three years to complete, and by the end of this time I'd be a complete wreck. So, I turned them down—which most people would consider to have been a disastrous career move. Consequently, I ended up working, in 1988, with the Kronos Quartet on the piece "Different Trains." In this piece, I'm using the strategy of playing the same note as the voice (of the train conductor) speaks certain words. This idea came as a kind of super-charged or turbo-charged epiphany, and the piece just took off and practically wrote itself. Afterwards, I thought to myself: "What if you could *see* the conductor saying the words? And with the music, the voice, and the visual presence of people onstage, or with video projections, you've got your opera!"

So, to answer your question simply: I'm interested in the human voice, and it's a very important part of my life and work.

NAN WATKINS: It's interesting that you mention the twelve-tone period and all that it encompassed, as I saw Stockhausen perform on his huge electronic apparatus when I was a student at Oberlin. We were dumbstruck with all this at the time.

And, then, one other footnote on the subject of classical music. I also saw Glenn Gould perform during those same years. I'd be interested in hearing what you thought of him as a performer/arranger/recording artist, as he, too, was playing around with stresses and harmonies and the human voice.

REICH: I think that Glenn Gould is the greatest classical performer of the twentieth century. In my mind, he has no competition. Bach's "Variations," which Gould performed, was one of my anthems when I was at Cornell. Yes, and as you point out, it's interesting that he saw that aspect of things—the voices, the counterpoint. As I say, it was all "in the air" in those days.

WATKINS: You're doing the world premieres for the two collaborative pieces "Bikini" and "Hindenburg" in Vienna. I studied piano in Vienna and Munich, and so I understand that environment. But my question is: Why is it that you're doing your premieres for these pieces in Europe instead of in America?

REICH: It's absolutely about money. You need to understand this. And the people in jazz should understand this, as well. I would venture that if you got Miles Davis, Charlie Parker, and John Coltrane together in this room, and you added up their tax returns, and added up how much money came from the U.S. and how much came from Europe, you'd see more European money. By the same token, if you got me, Terry Riley, La Monte Young, Laurie Anderson, Robert Wilson, and others together with our tax returns, you'd see that 85 percent of our income comes from Europe. In Europe they have tax-supported radio and television festivals. People in European countries actually pay for their radio and television privileges. If we tried to do that in America, there would be rioting in the streets. They're beginning to let that go, as the welfare state mentality is beginning to disintegrate in Europe.

So, if you're not one of the Three Tenors, it's much easier for American artists to go to Cologne than to go to California. And, what Europeans like about America is that which isn't imitating them. You see what I mean? They like their American artists to sound like Americans, not like third-rate Germans.

WATKINS: That said, do you see any evidence that Americans are trying to woo their artists back?

REICH: To the contrary. I will probably lose money coming down here, to Spoleto, which is one of the largest arts and performance festivals in the country. If I had to make a living making music in America, I'd do better to play music in the street.

WATKINS: Aside from our thinking of you as only a "product of your time," I also think of you as a philosophy major and someone who works off of ideas and subtle musical structures. We don't hear, so much, the kinds of melodies and harmonies in your work that seem to capture the attention of mainstream America.

REICH: I can't agree with that at all. While it may have been true for pieces like "Drumming" and some of the early pieces, for pieces like "Different Trains" and "Hindenburg" that's not true. If you didn't hear the harmony in "Different Trains," you didn't hear the piece. If you didn't hear the harmony in "Hindenburg," last night, you didn't hear the piece. Were you there last night?

WATKINS: Yes, I was there.

REICH: Well, I hope you heard the harmonies. I just want to make this clear, so we don't get stuck back in 1971 with this idea.

WATKINS: Okay, but what I want to get to is the idea of the dominance of the subtlety of rhythm and timbre—which seems to be reflective of an urban and a machine-age environment. Are you doing this in a conscious way, or is this more along the lines of what you were speaking of before as "a reflection of the times and the world we live in"?

REICH: I am who I am, and I'm doing what I'm doing. I'm not here to philosophize about anything at all, but just to present a new piece of work. While I might have been a philosophy student, now I see that discipline as being little more than an empty secular religion.

WATKINS: While you were at Mills College, there was a lot of electronic stuff going on there. My perception is that you've chosen to go pretty much with the acoustic form rather than to follow the fads and trends of electronic music that, say, composers such as Brian Eno have done.

REICH: Beginning in 1967 with pieces like "Piano Phase," we used all acoustic instruments with the exception of the microphone. Then, with "Different Trains," when the sampler keyboard came in, we used that. The way I feel about technology is this: that technology is interesting when technology can enhance what you've got in mind anyway. I'm not of the school that says: "Oh, here's a new gadget, let's try this!" And then just do whatever it is that the gadget does. We see this being done in rock-and-roll and in electronic music. I don't particularly care for synthesizers. I don't want a synthesizer that sounds like a violin. I want a real violin.

But with a sampler, this was a very different thing. You can bring in any sound, or any voice that you want and incorporate that into your piece. It's the composer who is driving the "different" train rather than the other way around, if you get my meaning. [Laughs.]

So, even though "Hindenburg" is a high-tech show, it's driven by the music that is played by people. The same can be said of the videos in the performance that are of real people, doing real things, and that have something to say about the whole piece, in general. It's not about "getting off" on technology. It's about using technology as a tool, an instrument, if you will, rather than a plaything.

WATKINS: Well, let me just ask you, then, who is your ideal listener? Someone who comes into a concert with a certain knowledge of your work or the subject matter and has some sort of expectations or intellectual concept going in, or someone who just lets the music wash over them and enjoys the music, allowing it to take them off into another realm? Or maybe a combination of both of these perspectives?

REICH: I would say that, for me, the ideal listener is someone who is really moved by the music. For me, the greatest composer who ever lived was J. S. Bach. The amount of technique this guy had is terrifying. But you can't just concentrate on that. And there's really not much you can say about his work. What matters most is that his music, or anyone's, gets to you emotionally. If it doesn't . . . well, we probably wouldn't be having this conversation, right? The emotional involvement has to come first, then we might find ourselves asking questions about other aspects of the music that are more cerebral.

WATKINS: You've had, at this point, a long and illustrious career. I'm wondering if there is any particular part of that career that you consider as being seminal for you.

REICH: Musically speaking, yes there is. And this is the idea of "canon." In the "Hindenburg" piece I set out to try something new. In the first and last section of "Hindenburg" there is an augmentation canon. It goes *da, da, te, de* . . . [Reich vocalizes the musical canon from "Hindenburg"]. As it gets stretched out, the whole feeling changes. There is some slow-motion stuff. [He vocalizes more of the canon "The Rise of Knowledge" from the same piece.] This is really an homage or tip-of-the-hat to the early-twelfth-century Parisian composer Perotin from the School of Notre Dame. He was the first composer that we know of to write in four parts. It's a kind of Gregorian chanting. He elongates each tone to five or six pages of written music. He's barely known these days. But his idea of the four parts and the stretching of the canon has really had a good deal of influence on my own work. I've loved a lot of the Medieval and Renaissance music since I was a music student. And so I've worked with many Early Music singing groups, particularly in London, over the years. And Ella Fitzgerald, too, who sings in this style, believe it or not!

WATKINS: You've talked about the arc of the "Hindenburg" piece in various publications leading up to its Spoleto performances. I'm wondering, then, how you would describe the arc of your complete work.

REICH: I wouldn't. [Laughs.] It's not my job.

CROWE: Let me just ask you, if you would, to elaborate on the idea of how your thinking and your music has moved from the philosophical to the spiritual over time. I think of Charles Lloyd as someone whose music has become much more spiritually centered as he has gotten older, for example.

REICH: I was born and raised a reformist Jew. In other words, I might as well have been a Unitarian. I had no knowledge of Hebrew, or anything else for that matter. Then, like many people of my generation, in the sixties, I got involved in yoga [Hatha Yoga] for a number of years, and in Buddhist meditation practices and TM [Transcendental Meditation]. It was all very good. With the exception of back injuries incurred from too much standing on my head. [Laughs.]

Around 1974, I connected with the Reform Synagogue in New York City and began studying biblical Hebrew, which is not the Hebrew which is spoken in Israel. I also began studying the Torah. All this branches out into the mystical and meditative sects of Judaism—which is experiencing a kind of rebirth these days.

So, I began studying all this stuff. I changed my diet. I avoided composing, playing and performing on Friday nights. I walked to places instead of riding—getting off the electric and electronic grids. All this as an attempt at being more in the spiritual moment. At least, as much as is possible. So, all this practice and all this meditation has made its way into my work and the way I think about my work. Aspects of "Sabbath music" have probably, in particular, become most evident at this point.

CROWE: Your music has been described, in fact, as being meditative. I'm thinking people are responding to the use of repetition, primarily. Would you go along with this assessment?

REICH: Well, that was the case more with the earlier pieces. With the later pieces it's a little bit less so. "The Cave," for instance, is a good example of this. We went around the country and asked the same questions (about Abraham the Prophet of the Old Testament Bible) to people of different religious persuasions and different ethnic and class backgrounds. The result is the edited "repetitions," if you will, of how these interviewees responded to our set questions. And, there is a kind of meditation in this process and in the final musical result. This piece is not about abstractions, but about what is actually happening with us, all over the world. So, I'd have to say that there is a practical and informative side to this piece, as well as the musical and meditative.

CROWE: My first introduction to the experience of the power of repetition came from my experiences and involvement with Native American drumming. I find your work as not being dissimilar to Native American music—which has, to my ear, very meditative qualities.

REICH: Yes. My piece "Drumming," which you heard tonight, is very much in that sound world, in that ballpark. And, yes, my music and style have changed, in some ways, over the years. For example, "Drumming," an early piece, is about an hour long in performance. The musical score is twenty-nine pages long. "Music for 18 Musicians" is also an hour in length, and it's about two hundred and thirty pages of musical text. Then, you have something like "The Cave," which is about two hours long and the score is about six hundred pages. So, you can see how things have become more complex, or intricate, as time has gone by. In the end, there's no such thing as progress in my music or in anybody else's. If anything, you could say that my music has become much faster. And not because I decided to do this, but because one changes as he/she gets older and starts doing things differently.

CROWE: What about making political statements with your work? With "Hindenburg" it would seem you're saying something political. Can you elaborate on this?

REICH: "Hindenburg" is part of a trilogy, which will include two additional works that deal with the two World Wars and the beginning of the Cold War. It's essentially about the twentieth century. It's about technology, but it's also about history. Hindenburg is a real character. In some ways, he defines the early twentieth century in Europe, if not also in the U.S.—as there was a very real historical connection between Hindenburg and Hitler, as we know well, today. And music, theatre or opera is usually *about* something. Something or someone in particular. In "Hindenburg" I'm interested in creating a kind of musical and visual documentary. But, at the same time, I don't want this piece to come off like a preacher. I'm not a preacher. I want the real thing. So, we're using historical footage and we're focusing on historical events. The early twentieth century is all about the build-up to World War I—so it's a very political time. Politics are definitely implied in this piece, if not directly addressed, as it's part of the times. And just like things were during those times, it's hard to ignore politics and the implications of technology in the world we live in today. As I work on these high-tech pieces with my computer, I also have a responsibility to bring up these kinds of issues and questions. Questions such as what is our responsibility, as humans, concerning issues of balance, sustainability and preservation of the planet and peoples, and species, that live on it. And this is what I am trying to do.

ARTISTS' DISCOGRAPHIES

PHILIP GLASS

Music with Changing Parts (1971)
Music in Twelve Parts (1974)
North Star (1977)
Einstein on the Beach (1978)
Glassworks (1982)
Koyaanisqatsi (1983)
The Photographer (1983)
Songs from Liquid Days (1984)
Dancepieces (1987)
Powaqqatsi (1988)
1000 Airplanes on the Roof (1989)
Solo Piano (1989)
The Thin Blue Line (1989)
Hydrogen Jukebox (1993)
Low Symphony (1993)
La Belle et la Bete (1995)
Heroes Symphony (1997)
Kundun (1997)
Symphony No. 2: Interlude from Orphee (1998)
Dracula (1999)
Early Keyboard Music (2001)

The Hours (2002)
Fog of War (2003)
Symphonies #2 and 3 (2004)
Orion (2005)
Symphony No. 8 (2006)
The Witches of Venice (2006)
Musique Pour Piano Solo (2007)

EUGENE FRIESEN

New Friend (1986)
Arms Around You (1989)
The Bremen Town Musicians (1994)
The Song of Rivers (1997)
In the Shade of Angels (2003)
Sono Miho (2005)

With TRIO GLOBO
Trio Globo (1994)
Carnival of Souls (1995)

With THE PAUL WINTER CONSORT
Missa Gaia (1982)
Concert for the Earth (1985)
Canyon (1985)
Earthbeat (1988)
The Man Who Planted Trees (1990)
Spanish Angel (1994)
Prayer for the Wild Things (1994)
Journey with the Sun (2000)

With MISCELLANEOUS ARTISTS
Reunion (1986) with Scott Cossu
Conferring with the Moon (1986) with Will Ackerman

Brazil (1992) with Toots Thielemans
The Romantics (1995) Various artists/Windham Hill
Celtic Soul (1996) with Noirin Ni Riain
Vacant (2003) with Dream Theater
Pure Water: Poetry of Rumi (2007) with Coleman Barks

CHARLES LLOYD

Forest Flower (1966)
In Europe (1966)
In the Soviet Union (1967)
Waves (1972)
Pathless Path (1979)
Big Sur (1979)
Tapestry (1979)
Montreux '82 (1982)
A Night in Copenhagen (1983)
Fish Out of Water (1989)
The Call (1993)
All My Relations (1994)
Canto (1996)
Voice in the Night (1998)
The Water Is Wide (1999)
Which Way Is East (2004)
Forest Flower: Charles Lloyd at Monterey (2005)
Sangam (2006)
Rabo de Nube (2008)

ABDULLAH IBRAHIM

The Dream (1963)
Duke Ellington Presents the Dollar Brand Trio (1964)
Anatomy of a South African Village (1965)

The Journey (1977)

Anthem for the New Nations (1978)

Echoes from Africa (1979)

Dollar Brand at Montreux (1980)

African Dawn (1982)

South Africa (1983)

Zimbabwe (1983)

Water from an Ancient Well (1985)

Chocolat (1988)

Blues for a Hip King (1989)

African River (1989)

No Fear, No Die (1990)

Desert Flowers (1991)

Mantra Mode (1991)

Knysna Blue (1993)

Yarona (1995)

Cape Town Flowers (1997)

African Suite (2001)

African Magic (2002)

A Celebration (2005)

SATHIMA BEA BENJAMIN

African Songbird (1976)

Sathima Sings Ellington (1979)

Dedications (1982)

Memories and Dreams (1983)

WindSong (1985)

LoveLight (1987)

Southern Touch (1989)

A Morning in Paris (1997)

Cape Town Love (1999)

Musical Echoes (2006)

SongSpirit (2006)

STEVE REICH

It's Gonna Rain (1965)

Melodica (1966)

My Name Is (1967)

Pendulum Music (1968)

Four Organs (1970)

Phase Patterns (1970)

Drumming (1970–71)

Clapping Music (1972)

Six Pianos (1973)

Music for 18 Musicians (1978)

Music for a Large Ensemble (1978)

Variations for Winds, Strings, and Keyboards (1979)

Tehillim (1981)

Vermont Counterpoint (1982)

The Desert Music (1984)

New York Counterpoint (1985)

Different Trains (1989)

The Cave (1990)

Typing Music (1993)

City Life (1995)

Proverb (1995)

Know What Is Above You (1999)

Three Tales (2002)

You Are (2004)

Phases (2006)

Works 1965–1995 (2006)

PHOTOGRAPHERS' CREDITS

PHILIP GLASS. Courtesy photo: © 2007 RichardPasley.com; used by permission of the photographer.

EUGENE FRIESEN. Photo by Sean Kernan; used by permission of Eugene Friesen.

CHARLES LLOYD. Photo by D. Darr; used by permission of the photographer.

ABDULLAH IBRAHIM. Photo by Manfred Rindersbacher; used by permission of Musikbüro.

SATHIMA BEA BENJAMIN. Photo by Motoe Shiratori; used by permission of Sathima Bea Benjamin.

STEVE REICH. Photo by Nevin Shalit; used by permission of the photographer.

THOMAS RAIN CROWE is an internationally recognized poet and translator whose work has been published in several languages. He is the author of twenty books of original works, translations, anthologies, and recordings, including *The Laugharne Poems*, written at the Dylan Thomas home in Laugharne, Wales, and published by Welsh publisher Carreg Gwalch; *Thomas Rain Crowe & The Boatrockers LIVE*, which received praise by such poet-musicians as Joy Harjo and Pete Townshend of the Who; and the award-winning book of nonfiction *Zoro's Field: My Life in the Appalachian Woods*, published in 2005 by the University of Georgia Press. As an editor, he has been an instrumental force behind such magazines as *Beatitude*, *Katuah Journal*, and the *Asheville Poetry Review*. His music articles, reviews, and interviews have appeared in many magazines, journals, and books in the U.S. and abroad. His literary archives have been purchased and are collected by the Duke University Special Collections Library. He lives in the Smoky Mountains of rural western North Carolina.

NAN WATKINS is a musician, writer, and translator who has degrees from Oberlin College and Johns Hopkins University as well as additional music study at the University of Munich, the Academy of Music in Vienna, and Tanglewood Music Center in Massachusetts. As a recording artist, she has appeared on several albums, including her solo recording of original keyboard compositions entitled *The Laugharne Poems* on the Fern Hill Records label. As a writer, she has published articles on music and the arts in many magazines and periodicals and written essays that have appeared in anthologies such as *A Woman Alone* and *Gifts of the Wild*. Her travel memoir *East Toward Dawn: A Woman's Solo Journey Around the World* appeared with Seal Press in 2002. She has translated and published the work of several German writers and poets, including *10,000 Dawns: The Love Poems of Yvan & Claire Goll* (White Pine Press, 2004). She resides in Tuckasegee, North Carolina, and is a member of the Asheville Area Piano Forum.